LIFE STRATEGIES, INC.

Life Strategies, Inc. was created to encourage individuals to embrace aging with enthusiasm, grace and dignity. Its purpose is to assist you in planning for retirement, the transition between work and retirement, and the continued enjoyment of a powerful, contented retirement. Life Strategies would be pleased to help you realize the best advantage of your life after work.

Life Strategies, Inc. provides written materials, seminars and personal coaching. If you would like additional information on the topic of retirement and optimal living based on your individual needs, contact us at (734)663-3151, or fax (734)663-0497. Information is also available at our website at www.life-strategiesinc.com.

PRINCIPLES

The life of an individual in retirement can be as good, or better, than pre-retirement life.

Aging well requires a balance between the physical, mental, social, emotional and spiritual aspects of life.

Aging well requires enhancing personal worth.

Aging well requires continuous learning.

Aging well requires a sense of humor.

Aging well requires a positive attitude about change and challenges.

Aging well means you can be sexy at any age.

Aging well requires staying connected to a community larger than you.

TABLE OF CONTENTS

ACKNOWLEDGMENTS

Writing this book about the aging process has been an important goal for me to achieve. This is a critical topic for me as I approach old age, and I think it's essential to learn as much as possible about new phases of life. I've been reading and paying attention to new findings about aging for some time, and I believe what I've learned can help others, as well as myself. This book is an effort to share what I've learned with you.

Aging with Enthusiasm, Grace and Dignity would not have been possible without the guidance, patience, suggestions, support and assistance of my partners in Life Strategies, Inc., Valerie Becker, Ph.D. and Francine Smithson, Ed.S. They have devoted a great deal of time and made innumerable valuable suggestions for improvement. They assumed responsibility for other aspects of the business to allow me time to write this book. I cannot adequately express my appreciation to them.

I also want to express my appreciation to all those who read early drafts and gave me important suggestions for improvement. Karen Kurple, Rita Foote, Renea Butler, and Liz Kobe were especially helpful and insightful. I am indebted to them for their time and for their thoughtful and discerning comments.

INTRODUCTION

Since celebrating my fiftieth birthday, I've been thinking more about the process of aging—what it means in our culture and what it means to me. With the numbers of people described by the adjective "aging" growing by leaps and bounds, I believe that many others are also thinking about the aging process.

Increasingly, research is being conducted to help us understand what happens to our minds and bodies as we age. The information provided by these studies needs to be readily available to all who are interested. This is what motivated me to undertake the compilation and writing of this book. I've attempted to review the literature and summarize the most important information and present it in an easily readable format.

A 1997 longevity and retirement study indicated that fifteen percent of the population believe that it is at least somewhat likely they will live to be 95. Forty-one percent say they could live to be 85. We are, indeed, living much longer than at any time in history. This increased longevity will have an incredible impact on life as we know it. If we have large numbers of people living long lives, we want them to be high quality lives. The alternative will lead to monumental costs in health care and supported living arrangements.

Fortunately, we are learning vast amounts about how to enhance aging so that the final decades of life do not have to be spent with diminished capacity. Individuals can learn how to improve the quality of their lives as they age and then develop plans to apply what they've learned. That's what this book is about. It is quick to read, presenting only the most important information, and in list form whenever feasible. It is a compilation of what we know about living life to the fullest as we age, tips for applying that knowledge, and a planning format to set goals and organize strategies to reach those goals.

The title for this book was given great consideration. I wanted it to convey a sense of how I believe we should go about aging—with enthusiasm, grace and dignity. Enthusiasm is a lively, absorbing interest or eager involvement. Grace is free unmerited love; beauty or charm; right and proper; or freely given. Dignity is nobility; worthiness; high repute, honor, loftiness of appearance or manner; self-respect. These, I think, describe exactly the right attitude for approaching and living through old age. We don't have any choice about getting older, but we do have a choice about the attitude with which we age.

As you read this book, keep notes in the margins and on the "Notes for Planning to Maximize My Life" page at the end of each chapter. In the final chapter you will find a planning form for each of the major areas of your life. Please don't just read this book and set it aside. Use it to develop a plan that you can use to improve the quality of your life.

After you've written your plan, make a commitment to follow it. A dusty plan will not help you achieve the results you want. My greatest wish is that you will use this book fully to help you create a happy and contented retirement and to age with enthusiasm, grace and dignity.

CHAPTER 1

AGING IN THE 21ST CENTURY

Recently, NBC did a television special celebrating its seventy-five years on the air. Besides being a great exercise in nostalgia, it was fascinating to see how the celebrities changed over the decades between the time their programs were on-the-air and the present time. There were visible changes in their hairlines, weight, skin texture, hair color and the energy they exuded. My first reaction was one of sadness to see the diminishment, especially as I confront similar physical challenges. Upon reflection, however, I realized that this is how our culture conditions us to think about the aging process. It is about decline and loss. It is about being less than we were when we were young. But it doesn't have to be that way!

Aging seems to be the only way to live a long life.
Daniel Francois
Esprit Auber
French Composer

Ancient cultures were far more adept at making use of the wisdom of their elders. They held them in high esteem—they revered and honored them. Use of their hard won wisdom and experience to advise the tribe in the course of daily challenges placed them in a position of dignity. Even though their bodies became more frail, they did not lose esteem.

In the United States, in the 21st century, we need to find ways to restore a measure of self-esteem to our aging population. **Medical advances have extended the life span significantly, but to what purpose if we live out our final years being considered of less value than we were in our youth.** "Agers" themselves have a responsibility to see to it that they attain this goal of giving more honor to themselves as they age with enthusiasm, grace and dignity.

We grow neither better or worse as we get old, but more like ourselves.
May L. Becker

1

Let's look closer at this concept of aging with enthusiasm, grace and dignity. Enthusiasm is lively, absorbing interest or eager involvement. Grace is free unmerited love; beauty or charm; right and proper; or freely given. Dignity is nobility; worthiness; high repute, honor, loftiness of appearance or manner; self-respect. These, I think, describe exactly the right attitude for approaching and living through old age. **You don't have any choice about getting older, but you do have a choice about the attitude with which you age.**

More people expect to live longer than at any time in history. A study on longevity and retirement done in 1997 showed that 41 percent of the people then working said they thought it was likely they would live to be 85 years old. Twenty-three percent said they could live to 90 and fifteen percent believed it likely they'd live to 95. [3]

People are living longer and need to plan accordingly to optimize their later years. This planning requires far more than financial planning. It must include all aspects of well being—physical, mental, social, emotional, and spiritual as well as financial. Taking responsibility for attitudes, behaviors, and planning will make all the difference. The most important factors in how we age are attributed to what we do rather than what is in our genes. **Having parents and grandparents who lived to an old age is important, but not nearly as important as what you do.** The decisions you make. The attitudes you exhibit. The extent to which you take care of yourself.

It is never too early, or too late, to begin to prepare for old age. For example, it is well known that obesity is hazardous to our physical health. We, as a population, have to take responsibility for what we consume regardless of how many ads we see for high calorie, high sugar, high fat, fast foods. Americans are jeopardizing our long term health for the questionable immediate pleasure of eating all those pizzas, bacon cheeseburgers, and doughnuts. There are no *good* excuses for overeating or eating poorly.

Recent research clearly shows us what we can do to age well and that is what this book is all about—reviewing and summarizing what we know about what we can do to

The way you think, the way you behave, the way you eat, can influence your life by 30–50 years.
Deepak Chopra, M.D.
Author

I refuse to admit that I am more than 52, even if that makes my children illegitimate.
Lady Nancy Astor
British Politician

improve the final decades of our lives. You don't have to do all this research for yourself. I've done it for you. And for me.

There is a chapter on each of the major areas in your life—physical, intellectual, social-emotional, spiritual, and financial. You'll be encouraged, and perhaps surprised, at how much the suggestions overlap. What is good for you physically is often good for you mentally as well, and maybe even socially and spiritually.

"Living quality lives as Americans grow older is defined almost entirely by individual financial planning followed by some level of acknowledgment of good health practices, but other lifestyle issues are rarely included in discussions related to longevity. Lifelong learning, volunteerism, care giving, leisure pursuits, second and third careers, and transportation involve issues which routinely impact on the lives of many Americans. However, most people do not readily identify that decisions made in these areas are an integral part of preparing for their future.

"Americans should understand the importance of planning for later life. By gathering information and developing strategies to ensure the best quality of life possible, individuals can ensure that as they live longer, they are also growing stronger."³

Life is a fatal adventure. It can only have one end. So why not make it as far ranging and free as possible.
Alexander Eliot

This is exactly what Life Strategies, Inc. is designed to do—to provide information and help you plan for your future well being. To assist you in aging with enthusiasm, grace, and dignity, not to mention good health in all aspects of your life—physical, mental, spiritual, social, emotional, and financial.

Many people are retiring earlier, maybe as young as 50. If you retire at 50 and live to 90 or even 100, you have a lot more decades of living to do. If you're going to be retired for thirty or forty, or even more years, it's important to consider what you want those years to be like? I don't want to play golf every day for 40 years. Life has so much more to offer. If I'm going to potentially live to be 100 (and that's my goal), I want to be as healthy as possible in every way possible. How about you?

Follow the advice of the experts—summarized here—

The wise man doesn't expect to find life worth living; he makes it that way.
Ancient Greek Proverb

Life is no brief candle to me. It is sort of a splendid torch which I have got hold of for a moment, and I want to make it burn as brightly as possible before handing it on to future generations.
George Bernard Shaw

and develop your plan. Exercise, eat nutritional foods, maintain a healthy weight, keep the mind active and alert, engage fully in life in all ways. While you're at it, don't neglect the hardest work of aging, the acceptance that it is natural and that you're privileged to be able to experience it. We have an opportunity that few before us had—living very long and healthy lives.

CHAPTER 2

STAYING PHYSICALLY FIT

- How much should I weigh?
- What is a healthy diet?
- What is the difference between good fat and bad fat?
- What kind of exercise should I do?
- How can I delay the physical problems of aging?
- Should I be worried about Alzheimer's?
- How does sexuality change with age?
- Should I take nutritional supplements?

In 1900, less than half of all Americans lived past 65. Life expectancy was about forty-seven years. Now, at the beginning of the 21st century, more than 80% can expect to live past 65 and well beyond. This graph shows how dramatically the percentages of older Americans are rising.[102]

I'm not interested in age. People who tell me their age are silly. You're as old as you feel.
Elizabeth Arden
1876–1966,
Beautician and
Businesswoman

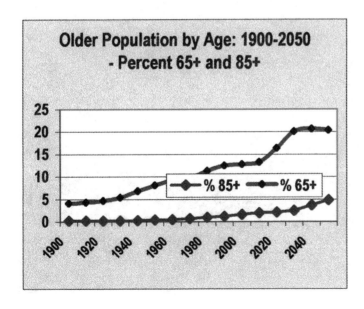

The most recent government study reports that life expectancy has risen to a new high of 76.9 years. This means that many, many people are living much longer than that. These additional years add what Gail Sheehy, in her book *New Passages*, calls a second adulthood. How you spend these bonus years is pretty much up to you. The attitude you choose and the decisions you make about exercise and nutrition make all the difference. Having extra years of life are, after all, not a benefit if you're miserable.

The very definition of old is changing. Not so long ago, we were expected to work until 65, live passively for a few years, and then die. No longer. Now we're retiring earlier and living many more years, maybe as much as thirty more years. And yes, that's a whole new adulthood. It is exceedingly good news that **no matter how old you are, it's not too late to develop healthy habits and improve your well being.** Of course, the earlier you start, the better.

Staying, or becoming, physically fit requires planning. Older people say that it is important to take care of their health, but the majority say they do not know how to prepare for a healthy old age. This book will help answer questions about healthy aging.

First, let's look at the top health concerns of those of us who are retired. Here's what we worry about:

1. Alzheimer's disease
2. Arthritis
3. Cancer
4. Diabetes
5. Heart disease
6. Hypertension
7. Incontinence
8. Loss of hearing
9. Loss of vision
10. Old age in general with the associated diminished capacity, aches, pains and osteoporosis

How concerned should you be about those conditions? What is it that kills us? Heart disease, cancer and stroke account for about 60% of all deaths. Chronic obstructive pulmonary disease, diabetes, pneumonia, and influenza also rank high in cause of death among the elderly. The conditions cited that don't kill us, affect the quality of our lives. Arthritis, incontinence, loss of hearing or vision, or pain can make it harder to enjoy the time we have left.

We can do something about it, though! We don't have to sit back and accept whatever happens while believing there is nothing we can do. We can take control of how we age!

TIPS FOR STAYING HEALTHY

There are three ways to view age. You have a chronological age which you can't do anything about. You can't change the date of your birth or how many years have lapsed since. You have a biological age and a psychological age. You *can* have an impact on those. If you pay attention to good health habits you can improve your biological age. And if you maintain a positive attitude and optimistic outlook, you can improve your psychological age. **You can choose to age with enthusiasm, grace and dignity.**

Today we know that we can do something about how we move into old age. We can take steps to slow and even reverse the aging process. Some important tips for staying healthy include:

1. Practice good nutrition.
   a. Eat nutritious foods that are low in saturated fat and sugar.
   b. Take supplements to further enhance nutrition.
   c. Give yourself incentives for doing well.
2. Exercise and include the three crucial aspects:
   a. Aerobic exercise strengthens the cardiovascular system.
   b. Weight training strengthens muscles and bone.
   c. Flexibility exercises lengthen and strengthen muscles to enhance movement.
3. Keep yourself intellectually stimulated.
   a. Learn new skills and habits.
   b. Continue to use or exercise your brain so it doesn't get lazy.
4. If you smoke, quit!
5. Associate with others who practice the healthy habits that you're working toward.

Most people think that aging is irreversible and we know that there are mechanisms even in the human machinery that allow for the reversal of aging, through correction of diet, through antioxidants, through removal of toxins from the body, through exercise, through yoga and breathing techniques, and through meditation.
Deepak Chopra
M.D., Author

You can free yourself from aging by reinterpreting your body and by grasping the link between belief and biology.
Deepak Chopra
M.D., Author

6. Visualize yourself the way you want to be.
7. Use alcohol in moderation and know the benefits of red wine.
8. Keep stress to a minimum. Practice stress reduction techniques, including:
   a. Meditation
   b. Yoga
   c. Self hypnosis
   d. Tai Chi.
9. Maintain a healthy weight.
10. Maintain a sense of humor.
11. Maintain a positive attitude.
12. Stay active!

When you get to my age life seems little more than one long march to and from the lavatory.
John Mortimer
British Barrister, Novelist

Ask yourself this question: If I continue to behave the way I'm behaving now, what will I be like in ten years? In twenty years? Of course, we can't know the answer with any degree of certainty, but we do know something about healthy habits and unhealthy habits. We know how much difference our habits can make in the quality and the length of our lives. Examine your health habits and project ahead to determine the likely outcome of those habits and practices.

There are three major areas in which you can make changes that will dramatically affect your overall physical well being—weight, nutrition, and exercise.

WEIGHT

What Do I Need to Know About Weight?

How old would you be if you didn't know how old you are?
Leroy "Satchel" Paige
1906–1982, Baseball Player

Obesity is a huge problem in the United States. According to the Center for Disease Control (CDC), more than sixty percent of adults in this country are overweight or obese. CDC also says that, "At least one-third of all cancers are attributable to poor diet, physical inactivity, and overweight." Seems to me that gives us some valuable information about what kind of good habits to establish, and maintaining a healthy weight is right up there in terms of importance. People who are overweight also have a higher risk for heart disease, high blood pressure, diabetes, and arthritis-related disabilities.

Take for example, Bernard, who at 62, was over-weight. Not obese, but he had gained about 35 extra pounds and his cholesterol and blood pressure were too high. He had developed the habit of eating whatever was handy to eat without consideration for health or nutrition. He liked fast food. Additionally, he was tired after work so he spent most of his evenings in front of the television set.

When he visited his doctor for his annual check up, he learned that he had several risk factors for a heart attack. Bernard, wisely, decided to take charge of his health. He ate more sensibly, he started to exercise and lost 32 pounds. Today, he is in better health than he has been for twenty years. He takes pride in how much better he feels and how much more enjoyable his life is.

What is a healthy weight?

Weight experts now generally use what is called the body mass index (BMI) to determine what is a healthy weight. BMI is calculated by using these steps:

I'd like to grow very old as slowly as possible.
Irene Mayer Selznick

1. Multiply your weight in pounds by 705
2. Divide the result by your height in inches
3. Divide that result by your height in inches again.

A healthy BMI would fall in the 20–25 range. A BMI of 25–29 is considered overweight, while a BMI over 30 is considered obese.

Body Mass Index Chart

BMI	21	22	23	24	25	26	27	28	29	30	31
Height					Weight						
5 ft.	107	112	117	122	127	132	138	143	148	153	158
5'1"	111	117	122	127	132	138	144	148	154	159	164
5'3"	119	124	130	135	141	147	152	158	164	169	175
5'5"	126	132	138	144	150	156	162	168	174	180	186
5'7"	134	140	147	153	159	166	172	178	185	191	198
5'9"	142	149	155	162	169	176	182	189	196	203	209
5'11"	150	157	164	171	179	186	193	200	207	214	221
6'1"	158	166	174	181	189	196	204	211	219	226	234
6'3"	167	175	183	191	199	207	215	223	231	239	247

There are a couple of other things that you need to consider in deciding what you want your ideal weight to be. One is that it may be okay to weigh a bit more than you did when you were in your twenties, if you still have a BMI of less than 25. Another is that where on your body you gain weight makes a difference to your health. If you gain weight in your abdomen, you are at a greater health risk than if you gain it in your hips and thighs. And, remember that weight is not the whole story. If you have a BMI between 20 and 25, but are sedentary and eat poorly, you could still be at risk.

To lengthen thy Life, lessen thy meals.
Benjamin Franklin

If you decide that you would benefit by losing a few pounds, remember how important nutrition and exercise are. As we age, our metabolism slows and muscle gives way to fat. Fat burns fewer calories than muscle further exaggerating the decline. It's not unlike an escalator that is going up while you want to go down.

NUTRITION

In twenty-first century America, you have unlimited choices about what you eat. Food of all kinds is available in great abundance. With so much food available you can easily find good, fresh, nutritious foods that will contribute to your good health. So, why don't you? Have you noticed that food and restaurant advertisements seem to be for unhealthy foods? Lots of high fat, low fiber, fast foods are quick and easy to grab when you're in a hurry. And aren't you always in a hurry? Even when you go into a nice restaurant for a leisurely meal, most menu choices are high in fat and calories. We seem to like our food fat and sweet, fat and salty or maybe just fat.

Drinking freshly made juices and eating enough whole foods to provide adequate fiber is a sensible approach to a healthful diet.
Jay Kordich
Health Expert, Author

Now is the time to make the decision, if you haven't already, to take charge of what you put into your body. Make nutritious choices. You already know most of what you need to know to make those healthy choices.

1. **Eat lots of fresh fruits and vegetables.** They are high in fiber, vitamins, minerals, and bioflavonoids. If you eat several hundred calories of fruits and vegeta-

bles each day, you'll be surprised how full you are and therefore less hungry for foods with less nutritional value. Fruits and vegetables with vivid colors tend to be the highest in nutrition. These include fruits such as strawberries, blueberries, cantaloupe, and raspberries or vegetables such as spinach, romaine lettuce, tomatoes, and broccoli.

2. **Eat a low fat diet.** No more than 30% of your total caloric intake should be in fat. Some sources suggest no more than 10%. And remember that one gram of fat has nine calories. This will help you calculate the percentage. Make the fat you do eat unsaturated or monosaturated fats. Monosaturated fats tend to reduce the low-density lipoprotein (LDL) cholesterol and raise the high-density lipoprotein (HDL) cholesterol. This means monosaturated fats decrease the "bad" cholesterol and raise the "good" cholesterol in your bloodstream. An excess of LDL in the blood is deposited on the walls of the arteries and causes hardening of the arteries. HDL takes the toxic waste, including LDL, from the cell to the liver to dispose of it.

To insure good health: Eat lightly, breathe deeply, live moderately, cultivate cheerfulness, and maintain an interest in life.
William Londen

Let me explain a bit more about fat. Fat is essential to a healthy diet. Fats are necessary for cell structure and the production of hormones. You must consume some fat. What you have to be careful about is the kind of fat you include in your diet. Types of fat include:

a. Saturated fats come mainly from meat and poultry products and tropical oils such as coconut and palm. These are unhealthy fats and raise LDL cholesterol in the body. You'll also find saturated fats in most snack foods and desserts.

b. Polyunsaturated fats come from fish and vegetable oils such as safflower, sunflower, corn, flaxseed and canola, and raise the HDL levels in the blood.

c. Monounsaturated fats are found in oils such as olive, canola and peanut. They are also found in avocado and most nuts and seeds. These fats raise HDL levels in the blood.

d. Trans fats are the those that result when vegetable oils are processed into margarine or shortening. These unhealthy fats are found in many snack foods and baked goods. You should avoid trans fats.

I don't eat junk foods and I don't think junk thoughts.
Peace Pilgrim
Peace Activist

3. **Eat more fish and less meat.** Fish (especially salmon, tuna, cod, haddock, herring, perch, or snapper) contains omega-3 fatty acids which raise HDL or "good" cholesterol. Meat is an excellent source of protein, but also tends to be high in saturated fat. It's probably okay to eat meat occasionally, but it should not be your primary source of protein. Other sources, such as beans and grains can also be good sources of protein. And fish is, of course, an excellent source of protein.

4. **Eat grains and legumes.** They contain lots of fiber and complex carbohydrates. They are low in fat and high in nutrition. Because they contain a lot of fiber, they'll fill you up more than "lightweight" foods. Be careful, though, about the amount of fiber in grains. Many products made from grains do not contain high amounts of fiber. Check the packages for grams of fiber per serving.

5. **Eat a variety of foods.** This gives you a broader range of nutrition, including vitamins, minerals, and fiber. It also gives you a broad range of flavors and textures to add interest to your diet.

6. **Drink tea, especially green tea.** Tea is high in antioxidants to combat the free radicals in your body that contribute to cellular destruction.

7. **Add soy products to your diet.** Soy came to our attention because Asian peoples, who eat foods rich in soy, have fewer heart attacks, are less likely to develop breast, colon, and prostate cancers; and suffer fewer hip fractures. Asian women also seem to have fewer hot flashes while going through menopause.

8. **Eat regularly. Don't skip meals.** This gives your body constant messages that food is available and it doesn't have to hoard it. Skipping meals causes your body to think it needs to retain the calories thus slowing your metabolism.

9. **Drink plenty of water.** You need at least six to eight glasses a day. This is important in keeping the skin more elastic, flushing toxins from your system, and it helps you feel full. It's easy to develop a water drinking habit. It is readily available wherever you go. You can even buy bottles of water from vending machines.

Take care of your body. It's the only place you have to live.
Jim Rohn Businessman, Author, Philosopher

Bottled water is easy to carry along wherever you go. Substitute water for soda pop—it has no sugar or calories and is consequently far better for you.

10. **If you consume alcohol, do so in moderation.** There is evidence that red wine provides some benefit because it contains antioxidants that combat the free radicals in your body. Excessive amounts of alcohol cause innumerable health and social problems.

11. **Consume only small amounts of sugar and salt or sodium.** They don't contribute nutritionally and may do harm to your body.

12. **Eat less and maintain a healthy body weight.** Obesity is a major contributing factor in many diseases. Some studies have shown that drastically reducing caloric intake in animals has increased their life span.

A man too busy to take care of his health is like a mechanic too busy to take care of his tools.
Spanish Proverb

You're familiar, I'm sure, with the Food Guide Pyramid developed by the U.S. Department of Agriculture. It gives general guidance about how much you should eat each day from each of the food groups.

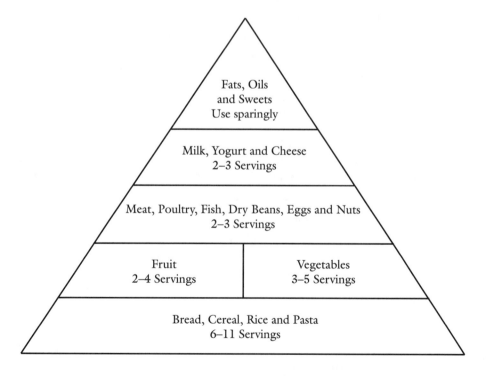

Fats, Oils
and Sweets
Use sparingly

Milk, Yogurt and Cheese
2–3 Servings

Meat, Poultry, Fish, Dry Beans, Eggs and Nuts
2–3 Servings

Fruit
2–4 Servings

Vegetables
3–5 Servings

Bread, Cereal, Rice and Pasta
6–11 Servings

Nutritional Supplements:

Much has been written about the value of nutritional supplements. The conservative point of view is that there is not yet sufficient research data to prove that they're effective. The prevailing view, however, seems to be that while there is not yet proof, there is compelling evidence that they do make a positive difference.

Supplements are particularly valued as antioxidants. Antioxidants help combat the free radicals in your body. That may sound somewhat confusing. Let me explain, briefly.

The molecules of your body are made up of atoms which are, in turn, made up of a nucleus, protons and electrons. The electrons participate in chemical reactions and help bond atoms together to form the molecules. When the atoms bind together, they create maximum stability for the molecule. When a weak bond splits, free radicals are formed. These free radicals attack other molecules and steal electrons, which causes these molecules to become free radicals and a chain reaction is started. Free radicals are a destructive force at the molecular level in the body.

The human body creates free radicals on its own but, they are also caused by pollution, radiation, cigarette smoke and herbicides found in the environment.

Antioxidants protect the body against free radicals by donating one of their own electrons to stabilize the molecule and stop the chain reaction. While the body creates antioxidants of its own, it may not produce enough to counter all of the free radicals in the environment.

There are foods that are high in antioxidants. Broccoli, fish, garlic, soy products, tea, and tomatoes are particularly high in antioxidants. Some, however, feel that we cannot eat enough to get all the antioxidants we need from food and that supplements are a good source for additional antioxidants. Vitamins E and C are particularly valued as antioxidants.

Nutritional supplements are believed to have numerous benefits:

1. **Vitamin E** is said to lower cholesterol, reduce the risk

As we free our breath (through diaphragmatic breathing) we relax our emotions and let go our body tensions.
Gay Hendricks
Psychologist, Author

of heart attack and stroke, lessen colon cancer, relieve arthritis, delay cataracts and brain and blood aging, protect the skin, and help maintain good health. Natural vitamin E is preferable to the synthetic form.

2. **Vitamin C** is believed to reduce artery disease, aid in preventing some cancers, lower cholesterol, stimulate the immune system, lower risk of chronic bronchitis, prevent cataracts, and strengthen teeth and gums.

3. **B vitamins** help maintain the ocular tissue especially the cornea and optic nerve; promote healthy skin, hair, and muscle. They support circulatory function and brain function and enhance energy. They also promote intestinal health and bowel function, liver health, and relieve moodiness or irritability. The B vitamins are actually a related group consisting of B1 (thiamine), B2 (riboflavin), B3 (niacin), B5 (pantothenic acid), B6 (pyridoxine), B7 (biotin), B12, (cobalamin), and folic acid (folate or folacin). It would be wise to take supplements as a B complex rather than attempting to balance the dosage individually.

4. **Calcium** has been found to strengthen bones and teeth. Additional studies show calcium to lower heart disease, and the risk for colorectal cancer.

5. **Coenzyme Q10** is used primarily to promote heart health. Recent studies indicate some promise in cancer prevention and AIDS treatment. Its effectiveness is being studied in relationship to use in several other areas but there is scant evidence at present to support its use for other purposes.

6. **Selenium** may help in the prevention of cancer, heart disease, and enhancement of healthy blood sugar levels.

Never hurry. Take plenty of exercise. Always be cheerful. Take all the sleep you need. You may expect to be well.
James Freeman Clarke
Minister, Theologian

There are some cautions that you should also know about if you're considering taking nutritional supplements.

1. You need less iron as you age. That is the reason that multivitamins formulated for seniors do not contain iron.

2. Both DHEA and human growth hormone (HGH) are getting considerable attention as a panacea for aging. If you believe the hype, all you have to do is take these hormones and you can reverse the aging process. Be careful. We know very little about the effect they can

have on adults and especially in pill form. If you're considering taking DHEA or HGH, consult with your doctor.

3. While beta carotene appears to block cancer, lessen clogging of the arteries, and stimulate the immune system, it is best supplied through the food you eat. There is some evidence that getting it through supplements can be dangerous, especially for smokers.

Nutritional supplements are being extensively researched. The evidence is encouraging, but still inconclusive. They appear to provide real benefit, however, you should not use them as a substitute for good nutrition. The greatest health benefits are still from eating nutritious foods on a regular basis. That means pay attention to what you eat all day, every day.

EXERCISE

As you age, your body converts muscle to fat. Fat burns fewer calories than muscle further slowing the body's metabolic processes. Now, doesn't that sound like awful news? Well, the good news is that you can do something about it. You can exercise. Exercise aids the body's metabolic processes.

You have to stay in shape. My grandmother, she started walking five miles a day when she was 60. She's 97 today and we don't know where the hell she is.
Ellen Degeneres

You can hardly pick up a newspaper or magazine today without seeing another article about the benefits of exercise. When you exercise, you may experience these benefits.

- more energy
- better sleep
- increased strength
- increased flexibility
- improved mobility and balance
- fewer falls
- decreased illness
- less anxiety and stress
- better mental function
- lower blood pressure
- less pain from arthritis
- better muscle tone

- stronger bones
- maintenance of a healthy weight
- enhanced cardiovascular fitness
- greater feelings of well being

A 1998 MacArthur Foundation study also indicated that exercisers had less chance of gallstones, colon cancer, diverticular disease, diabetes, osteoporosis, and enlarged prostates. When you exercise, you keep the body well tuned and functioning more efficiently and effectively.

If I'd known I was gonna live this long, I'd have taken better care of myself.
Eubie Blake [at age 100]
Composer

There is growing evidence that regular physical activity helps ward off mental declines as well as physical declines. In a five-year study of men and women aged 65 and older, researchers found that those who exercised regularly were less likely to develop Alzheimer's and other forms of dementia, and were less likely to see a drop in their mental abilities. The more a person exercised, the greater the protection for the brain.

It almost sounds like exercise will cure everything. Well, let's be realistic. Exercise won't cure everything, but it certainly keeps us healthier and slows the aging process. It is worth noting that exercise does not have to be vigorous to be beneficial. Even a thirty minute walk can be helpful for any age body and mind. And, you're never too old to start.

What Kind of Exercise Should I Do?

There are several different kinds of exercise for you to consider if you want to improve your health and flexibility.

1. Aerobic exercise raises the heart rate and improves the cardiovascular system. This includes rapid walking, jogging, running, bicycling, vigorous dancing, tennis, or any other activity that increases your heart rate significantly. You will perspire and breathe harder.
2. Weight training builds muscle and decreases fatty tissue. Studies have shown benefits for people of all ages, including some in their nineties. You can use weights, machines, or flexible bands to push, pull, lift or otherwise resist a force. This resistance helps keep your bones dense and your muscles strong, allowing you to be active and independent far into the future.

3. Stretching exercises improve flexibility. Yoga and Tai Chi are among the favorites and have helped millions maintain flexible muscles and joints well into old age. They also help reduce joint and muscle aches and pains. There are excellent classes and video tapes that show you how to do these movements and postures.

4. Meditation does not require muscle movement, but helps to calm the mind and increase the ability to focus. It is very difficult to quiet the mind and sit still, but there is evidence that it is extremely beneficial for both the mind and body.

There's lots of people who spend so much time watching their health, they haven't got time to enjoy it.
Josh Billings Humorist

When you're thinking about how to begin exercising, it's important to consider what you enjoy doing. Do you like to play tennis? Dance? Ride your bicycle? You'll get more exercise if you're doing something you enjoy.

It's also important to know what your limits are. It is wise to consult with your doctor if you're starting vigorous exercise after being sedentary over a long time. The idea is to improve your health, not to cause an acute problem.

Do you live near a gym? Do your public schools offer continuing education classes? Is there a YMCA in your community? Are there classes available for low impact aerobics, water aerobics, weight training, yoga, Tai Chi, or meditation? If not, there are plenty of books and video tapes, and even some TV programs available to show you the correct ways to engage in these exercises.

You may want to remember these tips.

1. **If it hurts, don't do it.** If you're doing something that hurts your knees, for example, you may need to modify the activity.

2. **Low impact does not have to be low intensity.** High impact activities can be painful on joints, but you can get the same cardiovascular benefit from doing low impact exercises.

A feeble body weakens the mind.
Jean Jacques Rousseau
Philosopher

3. **Wear the right kind of shoes.** Shoes are very important in protecting your feet and joints.

4. **Drink water.** You need to drink at least 6–8 glasses of water a day and it is especially important to drink water when you're exercising. Take a bottle along with you when you go for a walk.

5. **Be patient with yourself.** Don't expect immediate

success. Exercise is a process over time, so plan to keep exercising as long as you can move. Set realistic goals, meet them, and then set new goals. If you haven't been very active recently, start slowly. Just increasing the amount of movement you do is beneficial. Remember that being sedentary is bad for you; moving is good for you.

Heart rate is an important thing to know about. If you're going to exercise vigorously, you need to know what your target heart rate should be. To calculate your target heart rate:

1. Subtract your age from 220. This will give your maximum heart rate.
2. Count your resting heart rate, when you are sitting quietly.
3. Subtract your resting heart rate from your maximum heart rate. This gives your range.
4. Multiply .6 times your range. (You can use .7 if you've been exercising regularly and are in good health.) This gives your safe range.
5. Add your safe range to your resting heart rate to get your target exercise heart rate.

The concept of total wellness recognizes that our every thought, work, and behavior affects our greater health and well-being. And we, in turn, are affected not only emotionally but also physically and spiritually.
Greg Anderson
Wellness Author

Example:

Step 1	220	
	−65	Your age
	155	Your maximum heart rate
Step 2	75	Your resting heart rate
Step 3	155	Your maximum heart rate
	−75	Your resting heart rate
	80	Your range
Step 4	80	Your range
	×.6	
	48.0	Your safe range
Step 5	48	Your safe range
	+75	Your resting heart rate
	123	Your target heart rate

The sovereign invigorator of the body is exercise, and of all the exercises walking is best.
Thomas Jefferson
US President

When you do aerobic exercise, it is this target heart rate that you want to reach and maintain for at least twenty minutes for maximum cardiovascular benefit. A Harvard Alumni Study followed middle aged alumni over 26 years monitoring a number of variables, including exercise habits. The study concluded that those who exercised vigorously (jogging, swimming, tennis, bicycling) had a 25% lower death rate than those who were more sedentary or who engaged in non-vigorous activities (bowling, golf, strolling).

SUGGESTIONS TO GET MORE ACTIVITY INTO YOUR LIFE:

1. Remember that all activity burns calories. Just keep moving. Park at the far end of the parking lot instead of the closest space you can find.
2. Get up a few minutes earlier each morning and stretch. It will loosen up those tight muscles and you'll feel more like moving.
3. Ride your stationary bike while watching TV.
4. Work out with an exercise video.
5. Use the stairs instead of the elevator or escalator.
6. Walk to the far end of the mall when you go shopping.
7. Play active games with your grandchildren.
8. Put on your favorite dance music and move to the beat. Or, even more fun, go out dancing with your partner.
9. Practice good posture. Sitting or standing tall will help you feel better and look better.
10. Use hand held weights while you talk on the phone.
11. Do your own household chores if you've been having someone else do them for you. Remember that vacuuming, mopping floors, raking leaves, and cutting the grass are good for you.
12. If you'll do better with a friend, then identify an exercise buddy. You can help keep each other motivated.
13. Set a goal. What kind of exercise activity will you do? How often will you do it? How many times per week? How long will you do it? For how many minutes? Write down your goal.

14. Keep an exercise log. At a minimum, record the day and the number of minutes that you exercise. I use the following monthly log. I make up a page for each month and this way I can see very quickly how regularly I'm exercising.

DAY	DATE	ACTIVITY	TIME	DIST.	UPPER BODY	OTHER EXERCISE
Mon.	1	Treadmill	30 min.	2.3 miles	Yes	Weights Yoga
Tues.	2	Bicycle	45 min.	8.6 miles	Yes	Pushups Yoga
Wed.	3					
Etc.	Etc.					

To get rich never risk your health. For it is the truth that health is the wealth of wealth.
Richard Baker

That might be more information than you want to track, but I find it's a good motivator for me. And, since I prefer exercises that utilize the lower body like walking, running or cycling; I want to prod myself to pay attention to the upper body, as well.

If you have not exercised for quite some time, you might want to consider the exercises described in the book *Ancient Secret of the Fountain of Youth* by Peter Kelder. This book contains pictures and descriptions of how to do five gentle exercises that will do wonders to help you feel better and improve your flexibility. After doing them for awhile, you'll probably find that you feel good enough to do some other kind of exercise, as well.

SEX AND AGING

As we age there are some normal changes that occur, but perhaps not as many as are perceived in this youth-obsessed culture. The idea that aging adults are not, or should not be, sexual is outdated and just plain incorrect. Healthy individuals can continue to enjoy sex throughout their lives, even into their nineties, and probably beyond.

Normal changes in women include:

I'm at the age where food has taken the place of sex in my life. In fact, I've just had a mirror put over my kitchen table.
Rodney Dangerfield
Comedian

- Decreased estrogen
- Vaginal lubrication decreases, which may cause intercourse to be painful
- Fewer orgasmic contractions
- Rapid decrease in arousal after orgasm
- Vaginal walls may become thinner
- Vagina is less expansive
- Sexual tension may be less intense

Normal changes in men include:

- Erection may be slower, less full and disappears after orgasm
- Less volume of sperm
- Decreased production of testosterone (stabilizes at about 60)
- Size and firmness of testicles may be reduced
- Increase in size of the prostate
- May be an increased time before ejaculation
- Urgency to ejaculate is decreased

Health is a state of complete physical, mental and social well-being, and not merely the absence of disease or infirmity.
Heave

While there are some normal physical changes, research seems to indicate that other factors may have a greater impact on sexual expression as we age.

- Excessive alcohol use
- Depression
- Some prescription drugs
- Excessive obesity
- Lack of availability of a partner
- Chronic diseases (hypertension, heart disease, osteoporosis, arthritis, incontinence, diabetes, or emphysema)
- Surgeries such as mastectomy, ostomy, prostatectomy, hysterectomy, angioplasty, or heart surgery
- Reactions to changes caused by illness
- Attitudes towards alternative sexual activities when intercourse becomes impossible
- Performance anxiety

What everyone should know about aging and sexuality:

- "As one ages, the amount of sexual activity generally decreases, however, the amount of sexual interest and ability remains fairly constant.

- "If one's sexuality is constant throughout life, the biological changes associated with aging are less pronounced and sexuality is usually less affected.
- "Understanding that sexuality is normal and natural in old age is an important step to realizing one's own sexuality and becoming more comfortable with sexuality.
- "There is more to sexuality than just vaginal intercourse. There are many other forms of intimate expression ranging from holding hands, to kissing, to masturbation, to oral sex. Understanding that these options are available and acceptable can enrich sexual expression greatly.
- "Sexual activity is possible and takes place through the 70s and beyond! [Other sources say into the eighth and ninth decades.]
- " 'Sexual health' can be beneficial to the overall health of an elderly individual.
- "The physical exertion associated with sex is near the equivalent to walking up two flights of stairs. With this in mind, it is best to understand that sex for the patient of a heart operation would rarely be dangerous. (Consult with your physician concerning the risks associated with sex following a major heart surgery.)
- "Sexuality in later life is acceptable and natural.
- "If you have concerns related to health and sexual function (including drug interactions, chronic health problems, or surgical procedures) make a point to discuss these concerns with your physician or seek counseling and education from a therapist."[76]

Intimacy of all kinds is vital to a relationship, including sexual intimacy. In this example of Carolyn and Tom, sexual intimacy had ceased. They stopped engaging in sex in their mid-fifties and neither of them seemed to notice. Their days were full of outside commitments, their grandchildren and chores around the house. This lack of intimacy began to take its toll. They began nagging and antagonizing each other. Those in their company would sometimes grimace at their attitude toward each other.

When Carolyn was diagnosed with breast cancer and ultimately had surgery and extensive radiation and chemo-

You can set yourself up to be sick, or you can choose to stay well.
Wayne Dyer
Psychotherapist, Author

therapy, Tom became the caretaker for both Carolyn and the home. He was tender in his ministrations and Carolyn expressed her gratitude by being lovingly appreciative of Tom's assistance. Both of them realized how much they had missed the physical contact. The cancer challenge brought them together and reinstated their loving, intimate relationship.

While there are changes that may alter some aspects of the sexual experience, there is every reason to believe that aging adults can continue to enjoy physical intimacy throughout their lives. Maintaining good health is an important factor, but a physician may be able to help if you experience difficulties. A change in medication may be warranted.

Health is the greatest gift, contentment the greatest wealth, faithfulness the best relationship.
Buddha

Psychological or social factors may also play a role in sexuality for aging adults. Our culture seems to believe that its aging members are not sexually appealing. The assumption that sex is over for women when they can no longer bear children, or that men interested in sex are "dirty old men" is changing. However, these attitudes still exist and may affect the attitudes of older men and women. Not being familiar with the normal physical changes can cause both men and women to feel sexually inadequate as they age.

You might appreciate this light hearted story about sex and aging.

Margaret and Steven wanted to do something very special and unusual for Steven's father's one-hundredth birthday. Michael, Steven's father, has always been somewhat of a prankster and his children and grandchildren thought it would be fun to give him a dose of his own medicine for this auspicious occasion.

The family arranged to have a "lady of the evening" make a visit to Michael's residence on the eve of his monumental birthday. Michael was informed to be prepared for a birthday surprise that would arrive around seven o'clock in the evening before his birthday. Michael was admonished by his family to make sure that he kept in his hearing aids so that he would be able to hear the doorbell.

Promptly, at seven o'clock, the doorbell rang and Michael opened the door to find a beautiful, colorfully dressed young woman. "Yes", Michael asked, " May I help you?" "Why, yes", the woman smiled, "Happy Birthday, I am here to give you super sex."

"My goodness, dear", Michael responded, "I do believe that I will have the soup!"

After its introduction in 1998, Viagra has become the first line of treatment for men who experience impotence. The vast majority have successfully used this drug to overcome the symptoms of impotence. There are, however, some potential side effects that should be considered. The most common are headache, upset stomach, and flushing of the face. A small percentage of users may experience temporary changes in their vision including sensitivity to light and alterations in their color vision. If you have a heart condition, you should check with your doctor regarding the use of Viagra. There may be poor interaction between Viagra and some heart medications. While it is safe and effective for most men, there are good reasons that this drug requires a doctor's prescription.

Aging adults need to understand the normal changes and know they can continue to be interested, desirable, and capable. With some adaptations, you can continue to enjoy sexual relationships throughout later years. Some researchers have suggested slower but longer sexual activity which includes longer foreplay, more intense stimulation of the genitals, and the use of lubrication gels. Communication between the partners is of the utmost importance so that substitutes or alternatives can be used as needed or appropriate. It is also important to understand that intimacy can take on many forms, such as holding hands, hugging, kissing, touching. Sexual positions which compensate for physical needs, oral stimulation, non sexual relationships, psychological stimulation such as fantasy, and mutual masturbation have also been suggested. The bottom line is that you can continue to enjoy sex, but you may find an alternative way to do so.

To become a thoroughly good man is the best prescription for keeping a sound mind and a sound body.
Francis Bacon
Writer

ACTIVITY FOR PHYSICAL FITNESS

There are so many ways to increase the level of physical activity in your life that I'm reluctant to cite a single one here.

However, exercises for flexibility are, in my opinion, under utilized. When we think about being physically fit we are inclined to focus more on aerobic exercise or lifting weights. While those are essential forms of exercise, flexibility has an equally significant impact on how you feel and move. If your muscles are so tight that you can't tie your shoes easily or pick up something from the floor, it negatively affects the quality of your life.

To increase flexibility, try this simple set of stretching exercises:

1. Stand straight with your hands at your sides. Stretch your hands over your head. Reach up as high as you can and hold for a count of ten.
2. Repeat exercise number one, and lean to the left as far as you can and hold for a count of ten. Repeat, leaning to the right.
3. Stand straight. Clasp your hands behind your back. Raise your clasped hands as high as you can and hold for a count of ten.
4. Repeat number three, and with your hands clasped behind your back, bend at the waist as far as you comfortably can.
5. Sit on the floor with your legs straight in front of you. Reach for your toes, stretching as far as you can and hold for a count of ten.

Repeat each of these two or three times. Try stretching farther and holding for a longer count. These stretches will relax your muscles and increase the ease with which you move. They will also improve your posture and fluidity of movement. This will, in turn, help you to look and feel younger.

If these are easy for you to do, you might want to look for a beginning yoga class in your area. Flexibility is an important element in good physical health.

CONCLUSION

Virtually all the literature about aging and physical well being is consistent regarding the benefits of proper nutrition

If you don't do what's best for your body, you're the one who comes up on the short end.

Julius Erving
Basketball Player

and exercise. Seniors who pay attention to these factors are healthier than those who don't. They live longer and they live healthier. **It is never too late to begin to take better care of yourself.** Studies continue to show benefits for residents living in nursing homes when they add exercise to their routines. The earlier you start, the greater the benefits will be. So start now. Today. Commit to maintaining a healthy weight, eating a healthy diet, and exercising regularly.

If you have any questions about your ability to exercise or your diet, consult with your doctor. While some level of exercise is beneficial to virtually everyone, there are some physical conditions that would cause you to limit your activity or to progress more slowly.

Finally, visualize yourself as strong and healthy, then take steps to fulfill the vision. Picture health and vigor, not weakness or frailty. Your attitude makes the difference. We become what we visualize ourselves to be.

NOTES FOR PLANNING TO
MAXIMIZE MY LIFE PHYSICALLY

CHAPTER 3

STAYING MENTALLY FIT

- How can I maintain my mental acuity?
- Can I do anything to prevent Alzheimer's?
- Is a mature brain different from a young brain?
- Is there a relationship between physical aging and mental disabilities?
- Do nutritional supplements help the brain function?
- What does my attitude have to do with intellectual wellness?
- What activities stimulate the brain?
- What is the importance of genetic factors?

Perhaps the most common concern about aging is the loss of mental capacity or memory. In a recent Detroit Free Press column Desiree Cooper, the columnist, reflects on the nature of memory. When she was young, she said, forgetting was just something that you did occasionally. But as she gets older, forgetting takes on far greater meaning and worry.[40] We become increasingly concerned about whether it is normal forgetfulness, or is it the first sign of Alzheimer's? If I forgot to stop at the store on my way home from work, should I start worrying that I have Alzheimer's?

The art of being wise is the art of knowing what to overlook.
William James

How worried do I need to be about the vitality of my brain as the decades mount up? Is forgetfulness unavoidable? Will I inevitably have a decreased mental capacity as I age? Will I lose my independence when I get old? Or perhaps, do I worry too much?

You'll be glad to know that the answers to these and similar questions is amazingly good news. The short answer is that loss of independence and mental vigor are not inevitable. And, what you do, your health behavior, makes the difference. You can begin to take steps right now to improve your chances for mental fitness and alertness far into old age.

ALZHEIMER'S DISEASE

First, the facts. Alzheimer's is not a natural condition of the aging brain. It is a disease that occurs when a person loses the ability to think, learn and interpret because a protein called beta amyloid replaces normal brain tissue.[94] While precise numbers vary, the most commonly cited numbers on the incidence of Alzheimer's indicate that it affects about four million people today. That number is expected to grow to about 14 million by 2020 and to 22 million by 2050. These increases are expected due to the bulge in population created by the Baby Boomers and because more of us are living longer than in the past.

The percentages indicating the frequency of Alzheimer's are also hard to decipher. The best estimates seem to be that it affects about ten percent of those over age 65, and 30 - 50% of those who are 85 to 100 or more years of age. Other sources say one to two percent at age 65, 20% by age 80, and by 90 about 50% have some symptoms. What is consistent is that the risk increases significantly as we get older and older.

It is very good news that **your genes account for only about 30% of how you age**. What you *do* accounts for the other 70%. Dementia is not necessarily inevitable. Choosing a healthy life style can make a tremendous difference in whether you remain active and alert well into old age or become "old" at a young age. Remember that **Alzheimer's is a disease. It is *not* a normal condition of the aging brain.**

THE NORMAL AGING BRAIN

Now, that we've established that Alzheimer's is not normal, the next question is, "What is normal to the aging brain?"

I will never be an old man. To me, old age is always 15 years older than I am.
Bernard M. Baruch
1870–1965, American Financier

The greatest discovery of my generation is that a human being can alter his life by altering his attitude.
William James

It is important to understand the flexibility and compatibility of the human brain. The brain organizes itself. No other organ does that. The term given to this ability to reorganize and change over time is plasticity. This plasticity is what allows a human brain to repair itself after a stroke. Plasticity allows the brain to change its structure and function in response to experiences coming in from the outside environment. New learning and relearning can take place at any age and the brain changes in response to new learning.

The brain is continuously growing new connections between neurons or brain cells. These connections or synapses, made up of axons and dendrites, are what actually create the thought processes in the brain. It is these connections, established and strengthened over time, that allow for memories, learning, and problem solving. We won't get into the chemical and electrical impulses that power these connections. That's another discussion better taken up elsewhere. There is abundant resource material for you to study if you have a particular interest in how the brain works. The important thing is that scientists and doctors are continuously learning more about the brain, how it works, and how to keep it healthy.

The poor long for riches and the rich for heaven, but the wise long for a state of tranquility.
Swami Rama

There are normal changes that occur in the brain as it ages. These changes are not bad, they just make the mature brain different from the young brain. Changes are a result of a lifetime of experiences and learning and can make the "old" brain even more effective than the young brain. However, it would be good to remember that the 75 year-old brain is more like the 25 year-old brain than it is different from it.[136]

In general, attention span, everyday communication skills, many language skills, ability to comprehend, and simple visual perception do not decline. You can improve your vocabulary at any age. Some cognitive skills may decline including, naming of objects, verbal fluency, complex visual spatial skills, logical analysis, and selective attention.[38]

Types of memory change differently as we age. The ability to acquire, store, and retrieve new memories may be lessened, while the ability to retrieve old memories or those that have been stored and consolidated over long periods of time remains stable. Cognitive or intellectual abilities tend to peak during a person's thirties, plateau through their fifties and sixties, and decline during their seventies. However, this decline in the seventies varies among people.[38]

CAUSES FOR MEMORY LOSS

Everyone has memory lapses from time to time. There is no reason for concern unless these lapses become problematic in daily living. Serious changes in memory, personality, and behavior may be the result of a condition called dementia. Symptoms may include asking the same question repeatedly, becoming lost in familiar places, inability to follow directions, and neglecting personal safety, hygiene, and nutrition. Many of the conditions that cause dementia can be corrected or improved.

The tendency of old age to the body, say the physiologists, is to form bone. It is as rare as it is pleasant to meet with an old man whose opinions are not ossified.
J. F. Boyse

Depression is a common problem among the elder population and can affect your memory. The longer you live, the more likely that you will experience the loss of people close to you. There are constant messages that aging will result in the decline of your health and mobility, your mental abilities, and even your independence. Your income will generally be limited as expenses continue to rise. Depression is, perhaps, the most treatable of the mental illnesses. (See the end of this chapter for more information regarding depression.)

Stress, poor physical health, poor nutrition, and the misuse of medication can also affect your memory and mental function. High fever, dehydration, vitamin deficiency, and thyroid problems can also cause symptoms that mimic dementia. These conditions can all be treated and improved or corrected.

Alzheimer's is a common type of dementia and so far, there is no cure. There is, however, much that can be done to treat the patient and help the family cope. Sometimes drugs can be helpful, especially in the early or middle stages of the disease. Memory aids, such as notes, calendars, or lists, can be used to help the afflicted person cope in the early stages.

THE EFFECTS OF STIMULATION ON THE BRAIN

There are numerous studies that give evidence that mental function is not inevitably lost as you age. There are dozens of things that you can do to improve your prospects as you age, but taking a pill is not among them. There is no "magic bullet." If you want your brain to continue to serve you well, you have to take care of it, just as you have to take care of your physical body.

You are never too old to set another goal or to dream a new dream.
Les Brown 1945–
Speaker, Author

Mental stimulation causes the brain to grow more connections while lack of stimulation weakens the existing connections. "Use it or lose it" applies to the brain just as it does to the muscles of your physical body. Many types of mental decline are caused by lack of use of the brain. It gets lethargic because it isn't exercised, just as your body gets weaker if you don't get enough physical exercise.

Early education and mental stimulation are good predictors of mental fitness throughout life. However, this should not discourage those who did not have the benefit of a good education early in life. Mental training, even in old age, can boost intellectual power, help maintain mental functions like problem solving, and reverse memory decline.[136]

Studies have shown the following factors to be evident in seniors who maintain their mental facilities:

1. A high standard of living marked by above-average education and income
2. Lack of chronic diseases
3. Active engagement in reading, travel, cultural events, educational clubs and professional associations
4. Willingness to change
5. Having a smart spouse
6. An ability to grasp new ideas quickly
7. Satisfaction with their accomplishments.[136]

You can't help getting older, but you don't have to get old.
George Burns
1896–1996

Still other research found four key elements that were common among mentally alert elders:

1. Education
2. Strenuous activity
3. Lung function
4. Feeling that what people do makes a difference in their lives.[136]

WAYS TO MAINTAIN MENTAL ACUMEN

The resources on aging consistently cite similar strategies for maintaining and improving your mental faculties. Mental stimulation is universally cited, and there are numerous ways to get that mental stimulation. I've cited lots of things that you can do to keep your brain active and stay mentally alert. You'll probably find several that you use routinely. Select others that are especially appealing to you and keep your brain busy.

By the time you're eighty years old you've learned everything. You only have to remember it.
George Burns 1896–1996

1. **Maintain a positive attitude**. Don't let a negative attitude become a self-fulfilling prophecy. You will be able to do more and perform better if you believe that you can. Your outlook on life affects your mental attitude and your mental abilities.
2. **Take a class** that is challenging and interesting to you. Learn a new skill or strengthen an old skill.
3. **Play games**. Games like bridge, chess, or Scrabble are particularly good for mental stimulation, but lots of other games are also good for keeping you mentally engaged and interacting with others.
4. **Do puzzles** of all kinds. Crossword puzzles, jigsaw puzzles, logic puzzles, and visual-spatial puzzles are among the many kinds that will stimulate your brain cells.
5. **Nurture social relationships**. Positive social contacts are important for many reasons. They provide emotional support. They keep you engaged with others and give you opportunities to use various mental skills like memory, planning, debate, logic, and storytelling. Previous studies have pointed to marriage as enhancing longevity and quality of life, but at least one study

indicates that marriage may not be the most important relationship. "In a surprise finding from that study . . . unmarried adults appear to have higher mental functioning than married adults, and do not appear to differ in their mental abilities as they age."[96] Psychiatrist, Kenneth Sakauye, MD says that the finding of higher mental function among single adults supports the belief that what counts in social relationships is emotional quality, not quantity or marital status. "At some points in life your spouse can be your biggest support, and at other points can be your biggest burden."[96]

6. **Volunteer your time**. Get involved with a cause that you believe is important. This will give you a chance to use your brain and interact with others.

7. **Seek variety and challenge** in your life. Don't become too comfortable. Your brain thrives on variety and challenge. This is what the brain is designed for.

8. **Turn off the TV**. Watching television is relaxing and easy, and that's the problem; it's too easy. It has been said that eating a bowl of soup requires more mental activity than watching TV.

9. **Read.** Reading is a wonderful alternative to watching television. It's entertaining and informative. It is a great way to challenge your ideas and make you think. Reading requires more mental activity than TV because when you read, you have to make sense of symbols and create a visual image in your mind. And I know that you're a reader—after all, you're reading this book. You might want to broaden the scope of what you read to provide greater challenge and growth for your brain.

10. **Join or start a book club**. Discussions with others about a book that you all read is a stimulating and challenging way to read and learn from others. In addition, the social interaction will be great for you.

11. **Write** something. Writing is an outstanding way to force yourself to clarify your thinking, and believe me, it's mentally stimulating. Write letters to friends and family. You might even write your autobiography. What a gift that would be for your grandchildren—even if they're not interested now, they will be some day. What a great way to share your life and

The outer passes away; the innermost is the same yesterday, today, and forever.
Thomas Carlyle
1795–1881, Scottish
Philosopher, Author

experiences with your family. Or, you might want to consider writing poetry, short stories, or even a novel.

12. **Continue to learn** throughout your life. Never think that you know all that you need to know. You can learn new things by reading, searching the web, taking a class, or talking to others knowledgeable about a topic.

13. **Remain physically active**. Get lots of exercise. Walk, ride a bike, play with your grandchildren, take an exercise class, work in the garden, lift weights. Do something, anything, that keeps you up and moving! Physical activity stimulates blood flow to the brain and contributes to cognitive health. There is some evidence that the more exercise you get the better it is for your mental function.

14. **Avoid head injuries**. Drive a car with airbags. Buckle your seat belt. Wear a helmet when you ride your bike or engage in other activities in which you might fall on your head.

15. **Keep working at a job**. This doesn't have to be a full time job—you can do something part time. Work at something that will keep you challenged and mentally engaged.

16. **Eat nutritious low fat foods**. Potato chips, French fries, pizza, and cheeseburgers won't do it. Eat lots of vegetables, fruits, whole grains, and lean meats and fish. This is good for the brain as well as the body.

17. **Meditate or practice other stress reduction techniques**. Chronic stress alters brain structure and impairs cognitive function. Older people are especially susceptible to this effect. Meditation will also help you to practice maintaining focus.

18. **Seek help for depression** or other emotional disorders. Depression, in particular, is common among elders and deserves special attention.

19. **Sleep disorders are common and should be treated**. Sleep disturbances and loss of REM (rapid eye movement) that occurs while dreaming can impair cognition. If you have trouble sleeping, talk with your doctor about potential remedies.

20. **Effectively control high blood pressure, diabetes, high cholesterol, and other medical ailments**. Poor

Childhood itself is scarcely more lovely than a cheerful, kindly, sunshiny old age.
Lydia M. Child
1802–1880, American
Abolitionist, Writer, Editor

physical health can have a detrimental effect on the brain.

21. **Learn something entirely new** like playing a musical instrument, ballroom dancing, painting, knitting, how to use a computer or the internet. Just make it something that is new to you and a challenge. You'll want to select something that you'll enjoy, so you'll work harder at it and stick with it longer. New learning grows new brain connections—new learning grows brain.

22. **Go to the library.** Investigate new areas. Browse in an area of the library that you might not have thought about before. You can do pretty much the same thing in a bookstore, but the library is cheaper. Additionally, the library will have computers that you can use and resource people to help you.

There is probably no way you can get too much mental stimulation. You might start by adding some items to this list that I didn't find in the literature or think of myself. If an activity challenges your brain—makes you think—it's good for maintaining or strengthening your mental capacity.

Every stage of human life, except the last, is marked out by certain and defined limits; old age alone has no precise and determinate boundary.
Marcus T. Cicero
c. 106–43 BC, Great Roman Orator, Politician

SUPPLEMENTS AND THE BRAIN

Wouldn't it be nice . . . if you could just take a pill and have a guarantee that your brain wouldn't deteriorate on you? Well, it isn't as easy as that. Scientists are looking hard and they're learning some very interesting things about our brains, but so far, there is no conclusive evidence that a pill, or tablet, or capsule will solve the problem.

Depending on what you read and who wrote it, some great claims are being made about ginkgo biloba, vitamin E, selegiline, vitamin C, estrogen, DHEA, pregnenolone, nonsteroidal anti-inflammatory drugs (NSAIDs) and others.

A year-long study published in the Journal of the American Medical Association studied 309 patients with dementia caused by loss of blood to the brain. Those who were given ginkgo biloba showed modest improvements on mental and behavioral tests over test subjects who were given a placebo. It is theorized that ginkgo biloba is an antioxidant that reduces the stickiness of blood platelets, increases blood flow to the brain and thus reduces the deterioration of the brain. This supplement is generally considered to be safe when taken in the recommended dosages.[79]

Some studies have indicated that NSAIDs reduce the risk of Alzheimer's. NSAIDs include ibuprofen (Advil, Motrin, Nuprin), naproxen sodium (Aleve), and indomethacin (Indocin). These drugs, in at least one long-term study, reduced the risk by thirty to sixty percent. Asprin and acetaminophen (Tylenol) did *not* have the same effect. NSAIDs are taken by many people for chronic conditions such as arthritis. They are not, however, recommended for mental function because they can have serious side effects such as gastrointestinal bleeding. Stronger evidence is needed before they will be recommended to improve your chances of avoiding Alzheimer's.

Old age, especially an honored old age, has so great authority, that this is of more value than all the pleasures of youth.
Marcus T. Cicero
c. 106–43 BC, Great
Roman Orator, Politician

Vitamins E and C are antioxidants, as is selegiline (which is used for treating Parkinson's disease). Antioxidants are thought to prevent nerve cell damage by destroying free radicals which are created normally in the body as a byproduct of cell metabolism and are increased by environmental factors. Some studies give evidence that these antioxidants are useful in delaying the onset of dementia, especially vascular dementia which is the second most common kind following Alzheimer's.

Estrogen has shown some promising results. It is suspected that the loss of estrogen in the body is a contributing factor in women being more susceptible to Alzheimer's than men. Some studies have shown that estrogen replacement therapy following menopause reduces a woman's risk for Alzheimer's disease. Studies have also indicated that estrogen replacement can improve mental abilities in women who have developed Alzheimer's disease.

However, the evidence is not solid enough, at this time, to suggest the use of estrogen therapy for prevention or treatment of this disease. At least one long term study of hormone replacement therapy was recently discontinued earlier than anticipated because an increased risk of breast cancer, strokes and other conditions were indicated. The lesson is, I think, that a great deal more study is required before we can feel safe using estrogen to circumvent the signs of aging.

Furthermore, estrogen alternatives such as raloxifene (Evista) showed little evidence of an effect on cognitive function. They are effective substitutes for preventing osteoporosis, but apparently not for preventing dementia.

The logical conclusion to draw is that it is premature to take any pill or nutritional supplement to prevent any form of dementia. However, you might want to examine the other benefits of some of the things under study. Cognitive health is related to physical health, and it can't hurt to improve your overall physical well being. In doing so, you will want to be especially conscious of any potential negative side effects. Remember that researchers and medical practitioners are justifiably cautious in recommending any substance that has not been proven to be effective. That is as it should be. Individuals may, however, study potential risks and benefits and make their own informed decisions. Do what you think is best for you.

Father Time is not always a hard parent, and, though he tarries for none of his children, often lays his hand lightly upon those who have used him well; making them old men and women inexorably enough, but leaving their hearts and spirits young and in full vigor. With such people the gray head is but the impression of the old fellow's hand in giving them his blessing, and every wrinkle but a notch in the quiet calendar of a well-spent life.
Charles Dickens
1812–1870, British
Novelist

ASSESSING YOUR RISK FOR ALZHEIMER'S

There are only two well documented factors that increase your risk for Alzheimer's Disease (AD): advancing age and heredity.

As people get older, more of them get Alzheimer's. This increase goes from less than five percent at age 65 to about twenty percent at age 80, and by 90 about fifty percent have some symptoms. Alzheimer's disease rarely affects those under 65 years of age. Women are more susceptible than men, at least in part because they tend to live longer.

Heredity plays a larger role in early onset Alzheimer's than it does in individuals in which AD begins at older ages. About forty percent of those who get the disease before age 65 have a family history of doing so. Only about three percent of all cases (early onset and older ages) have been demonstrated to have a heredity link. Even in families with several members who have had Alzheimer's, most family members don't get the disease. The genetic connection in the more typical late onset (after age 65) is being linked to one of the genes for apolipoprotein E (ApoE). Researchers are seeking ways to block the action of this gene (ApoE4), improve treatments, and prevent AD in those who carry it. Not everyone who has this gene will get AD, but about a third of all early onset cases appear to be linked to ApoE4.

While there does appear to be a genetic link, it is not worth worrying about. For example, Laura has worried since middle age that she would have Alzheimer's Disease or some form of dementia just as her mother and grandmother did. Laura has not been tested for a hereditary link, but has been concerned about the family pattern. However, at 84, she remains physically fit and mentally alert, as do her siblings. She exemplifies the futility of worrying about something that may never happen.

It is not how old you are, but how you are old.
Marie Dressler
1869–1934, Canadian
Stage and Film Actor

Other factors are being studied and are suspected to be linked to AD, but no link has yet been proven.

Environmental factors are being studied as possible causes of AD. Among these are aluminum and zinc because the brain tissue of some AD victims show traces of these elements. Thus far, no clear link has been proven between these or other metals and AD.

African-Americans have a higher incidence of high blood pressure. This may contribute to a higher occurrence of vascular dementia and account for an increased risk of dementia for this group. Vascular dementia is caused by blood vessels to the brain becoming narrowed or blocked.

I'm saving that rocker for the day when I feel as old as I really am.
Dwight D. Eisenhower
1890–1969, Thirty-fourth
President of the USA

Mental fitness is also under study. Generally health practitioners believe that good mental and physical health will improve the quality of life. Thus far, research has not proven that mental or physical fitness will prevent AD or even reduce the risk.

There is conflicting research evidence regarding such

factors as severe head trauma, viruses, family history of Down syndrome, thyroid disease and smoking. These deserve further study.

SYMPTOMS

As we age our brains undergo normal changes. The numbers of cells, or neurons, decrease as do the number of dendrites that branch off from the cells. The number of amyloid plaques increases. These changes affect cognitive function remarkably little and the individual will not be aware of these changes.

In the Alzheimer's diseased brain, there is an overall shrinkage of the brain tissue, amyloid plaques increase, and there are growing numbers of neurofibrillary tangles. The amyloid plaques are protein fragments, produced normally by the body, that accumulate between the nerve cells, or neurons, of the brain. Neurofibrillary tangles are twisted fibers inside the brain cells which interfere with the transporting of nutrients and other important substances within the brain.[9]

A concern for loss of mental ability may be nearly universal. Throughout life we experience forgetfulness to some extent, but as we age we worry about it more. The Alzheimer's Association cites some symptoms that will help guide you in determining whether there is cause for genuine concern. These should not be construed to mean that you or someone you love does, or does not, have Alzheimer's, but they can serve as a useful guide. This list was adapted from one provided by Alzheimer's Association.

1. **Memory Loss** of recently acquired information is one of the most commonly recognized early signs of dementia. People of all ages forget things sometimes, such as names, appointments or phone numbers, but those with dementia forget more often and don't remember them later.
2. **Difficulty Performing Familiar Tasks**. A person with Alzheimer's may not know how to prepare a meal, use a household appliance, or perform a hobby

An important antidote to American democracy is American gerontocracy. The positions of eminence and authority in Congress are allotted in accordance with length of service, regardless of quality. Superficial observers have long criticized the United States for making a fetish of youth. This is unfair. Uniquely among modern organs of public and private administration, its national legislature rewards senility.
John Kenneth Galbraith 1908–, American Economist

Seek ye counsel of the aged for their eyes have looked on the faces of the years and their ears have hardened to the voices of Life. Even if their counsel is displeasing to you, pay heed to them.
Kahlil Gibran
1883–1931, Lebanese
Poet, Novelist

The worst old age is that of the mind.
William Hazlitt
1778–1830, British Essayist

they've engaged in for decades. These everyday tasks that we do automatically may be extremely difficult for someone with AD.

3. **Problems with Language**. Those with Alzheimer's may forget simple words or substitute unusual words in sentences. For example, when unable to find their shoes they may ask for those things for their feet. This is considerably more problematic than the typical forgetting of a word that we all experience occasionally.

4. **Disorientation to Time and Space**. Alzheimer's victims may become lost on their own street, forget where they are and how they got there, and not know how to get back home.

5. **Poor or Decreased Judgment**. While everyone displays poor judgment occasionally, those with Alzheimer's routinely exhibit this trait. They may do things such as wear several sweaters in warm weather or shorts and sandals in the snow. They may also spend money they cannot afford by giving it to telemarketers or purchasing home repairs they don't need. One specific story is cited about a man who needed a new refrigerator, so he ordered a new one—every day for twelve days. The store finally contacted his family to see what was happening.

6. **Problems with Abstract Thinking**. Balancing a checkbook, for example, would be extremely problematic if you completely forgot what numbers are and what you are supposed to do with them.

7. **Misplacing Things**. A person with Alzheimer's may put things in unusual places. For example, an iron in the freezer, a wristwatch in the sugar bowl, or a sandwich under the sofa.

8. **Changes in Mood or Behavior**. While anyone can exhibit mood changes, someone with AD may display rapid and extreme mood swings for no apparent reason.

9. **Changes in Personality**. A person with AD may become extremely confused, suspicious, fearful, or dependent on a family member.

10. **Loss of Initiative**. Someone with AD may become very passive, sitting in front of the television for hours, sleeping more than usual, or not wanting to do their usual activities.

If these symptoms are present, it would be wise to have a thorough medical examination. Considerable progress is being made in the diagnosis of Alzheimer's and other forms of dementia, but it cannot be confirmed without an autopsy of the brain. The Alzheimer's Association cites four drugs approved by the FDA that are used for treatment of Alzheimer's disease. They include tacrine (Cognex), donepezil (Aricept), rivastigmine (Exelon), and galantamine (Reminyl). Several others are being tested. While there is no cure, progress is being made in management of the disease and support for the family.

Few people know how to be old.
Francois De La Rochefoucauld
1613–1680, French Classical Writer

MENTAL FITNESS ACTIVITY

This is not a test for Alzheimer's; it is an activity to challenge your brain and help keep it fit.

Place ten coins or disks on a table arranged as indicated here.

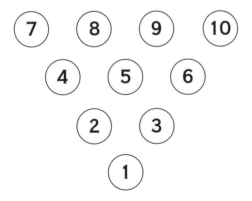

Move only three coins or disks to turn the triangle upside down. (See page 48 for the solution.)

DEPRESSION AND AGING

Approximately fifteen percent of the population over age sixty-five may suffer from depression. That's about five million people. This makes depression the most prevalent mental health issue among the elderly. Fortunately, it is also the most treatable mental illness.

Everyone feels "down" or "blue" from time-to-time throughout life. There are events that cause us to feel sad, such as the loss of someone we love, or the end of an important relationship. Situational or temporary sadness are not the same as clinical depression. Depression can also be the result of a chronic medical condition or medication.

Researchers who study depression have found that the amygdala and the hypothalamus (parts of the brain) are affected by stress or upsetting conditions. The amygdala and the hypothalamus, under stress, create a chemical chain reaction that leads to depression. It is believed that decreased amounts of serotonin and other neurotransmitters are linked to sleep problems, irritability, anxiety, fatigue, and despondency that are associated with depression.[28]

"Chronic or serious illness is the most common cause of depression in the elderly. However, the disease also can be caused by biological changes in the brain and, thus, may occur for no visibly apparent reason. As the body and brain age, a number of bio-chemical changes begin to take place. Changes as the result of aging, medical illness or genetics may put the older adult at a greater risk for developing depression."[41]

Some symptoms of depression that you may want to be alert for, include:

- Sadness that doesn't go away
- Loss of interest in your job, family life, or social activities, other things that you previously enjoyed
- Physical pain that seems to have no cause
- Sleep disturbances
- Slowed thinking or response
- Excessive worry about finances, health, or other matters
- Tearfulness that you can't explain
- Unusual irritability
- Attitude of indifference or loss of self-esteem
- Feelings of worthlessness or helplessness
- Weight changes
- Loss of concentration

Old men are fond of giving good advice to console themselves for their inability to give bad examples.
Francois De La Rochefoucauld 1613–1680, French Classical Writer

A man is not old as long as he is seeking something.
Jean Rostand 1894–1977 French Biologist, Writer

- Staring off into space (or at the television) for prolonged periods of time
- Suicidal thoughts

If you are concerned that you, or someone close to you, may be suffering from depression, you might find this quiz from the National Council on Aging and the American Association for Geriatric Psychiatry to be useful.[70]

GERIATRIC DEPRESSION SCALE

Choose the best answer for how you felt over the past week. Please check one:

		Yes	No
1.	Are you basically satisfied with life?	☐	☐
2.	Have you dropped many of your activities and interests?	☐	☐
3.	Do you feel that your life is empty?	☐	☐
4.	Do you often get bored?	☐	☐
5.	Are you in good spirits most of the time?	☐	☐
6.	Are you afraid that something bad is going to happen to you?	☐	☐
7.	Do you feel happy most of the time?	☐	☐
8.	Do you often feel helpless?	☐	☐
9.	Do you prefer staying at home to going out and doing things?	☐	☐
10.	Do you feel you have more problems with memory than most people?	☐	☐
11.	Do you think it is wonderful to be alive now?	☐	☐
12.	Do you feel pretty worthless the way you are now?	☐	☐
13.	Do you feel full of energy?	☐	☐
14.	Do you feel that your situation is hopeless?	☐	☐
15.	Do you think that most people are better off than you are?	☐	☐

One is rarely an impulsive innovator after the age of sixty, but one can still be a very fine orderly and inventive thinker. One rarely procreates children at that age, but one is all the more skilled at educating those who have already been procreated, and education is procreation of another kind.

Georg C. Lichtenberg 1742–1799, German Physicist, Satirist

Scoring: Give yourself one point for each of the following answers. A score of 0–5 is normal; a score above 5 suggests depression.

I have found it to be true that the older I've become the better my life has become.
Rush Limbaugh 1951–,
American TV Personality

1. No	4. Yes	7. No	10. Yes	13. No
2. Yes	5. No	8. Yes	11. No	14. Yes
3. Yes	6. Yes	9. Yes	12. Yes	15. Yes

The psychoanalyst, Erik Erikson, viewed the final stages of life as the period in which we come to terms with who and what we are; the time to acknowledge our accomplishments and to integrate what we've learned throughout life. He believed that when we do this successfully, we achieve what he labeled integrity. The inability to do this leads to despair. He viewed integrity as knowing who we are and accepting ourselves fully so we can live out our lives with a sense of completeness. Depression interferes with the achievement of this integrity and contributes to the other end of the scale—despair.

Treatments for depression include medication, psychotherapy, and in extreme cases electroconvulsive (ECT) therapy. Medication can ameliorate the effects of a chemical imbalance in the brain. Psychotherapy is most helpful when the depression is the result of life circumstances such as, loss of someone or something that we care about; low self-esteem, or relationship problems.

ECT consists of a series of six to twelve treatments in which electrodes are placed on the head to deliver a small and painless electrical stimulus to the brain. This stimulates the brain to produce more of the chemicals that are in short supply. ECT is typically used only when other therapies have not been effective or rapid relief is required. It has been demonstrated to be extremely effective.

I like spring, but it is too young. I like summer, but it is too proud. So I like best of all autumn, because its tone is mellower, its colors are richer, and it is tinged with a little sorrow. Its golden richness speaks not of the innocence of spring, nor the power of summer, but of the mellowness and kindly wisdom of approaching age. It knows the limitations of life and its content.
Lin Yü-tang
1895–1976, Chinese
Writer and Philologist

Depression is common and treatable. It is nothing to be embarrassed about. If you, or someone you love, exhibits signs of depression don't hesitate to seek relief. See your doctor, starting with your primary care physician.

CONCLUSION

Fear of dependence, in the elderly, is caused by concerns about both physical and mental wellness. Alzheimer's is perhaps the greatest fear, but loss of mobility, vision, and/or hearing can also cause great dread.

Recent research in both biological and psychological fields has confirmed that:

1. "Genetic factors account for only about half of general mental ability in later life. There is substantial room for non-genetic, i.e., lifestyle, measures to improve mental ability.

2. "Education is the strongest predictor of sustained mental function. Education early in life may have a direct beneficial effect on brain circuitry. It may also set a pattern of intellectual activities which when exercised later in life serves to maintain cognitive function.

3. "Physical exercise and lung function enhance the function of the central nervous system, especially memory function.

4. "A sense of self-efficacy—the belief that one can accomplish tasks—leads to improved performance of many kinds involving cognitive function. Self-efficacy has an effect on memory and successful efforts reinforce the underlying sense of self-efficacy. On the other hand, low self-esteem reinforces resignation, lack of effort and downward spiral of unused abilities.

5. "Complex environments provide a variety of stimuli, choice and opportunities that exercise and sustain mental function.

6. "Mental function can be significantly improved by appropriate training and practice, even among older adults who showed a clear decline in certain cognitive functions, including memory loss.

7. "Social support has a positive effect on mental performance in older age."[86]

You can judge your age by the amount of pain you feel when you come in contact with a new idea.
John Nuveen

I venerate old age; and I love not the man who can look without emotion upon the sunset of life, when the dusk of evening begins to gather over the watery eye, and the shadows of twilight grow broader and deeper upon the understanding.
Henry Wadsworth Longfellow 1819–1892, American Poet

Recent research shows that brain cells can be regenerated in the hippocampus, which is an area of the brain that is important to the establishment of new memories and information.

Simon Fraser University, conducting research in collaboration with Century House Association, studied the effect of mental fitness programs on older adults. They developed a series of day-long mental fitness workshops. In these workshops, participants learned:

1. How old attitudes and beliefs about declining mental abilities limited their options as they aged,

There is a fountain of youth: it is your mind, your talents, the creativity you bring to your life and the lives of the people you love. When you learn to tap into this source, you will truly have defeated age.
Sophia Loren
1934–, Italian Film Actress

2. How to change those limiting beliefs to positive beliefs about what they could do in old age,
3. How to speak the language of limitless possibility,
4. How to think differently and creatively—"out of the box",
5. To appreciate diversity and differing views of the world, and
6. To listen to others for understanding and with respect.

Follow-up tests revealed that participants in these workshops showed improved performance on cognitive tests.[86] There is something you can do to increase your chances of remaining active and alert in old age!

It might serve you well to focus on growing into wisdom. You can do this by drawing on your many life experiences. Reflect on what you've learned. It isn't your job to teach it to the world—to impose on others your lifetime of learning—but to share your reflections as appropriate. That is appropriate and helpful to others, not to you. Wisdom does not impose itself on others, but is offered in a loving way.

Solution to the Mental Fitness Activity on page 43:
Move disks 7 and 10 to the third row; move disk 1 to the top.

NOTES FOR PLANNING TO MAXIMIZE MY LIFE MENTALLY

CHAPTER 4

THE ROLE OF SPIRITUALITY

- Is there a difference between religion and spirituality?
- Will spirituality help me live longer?
- How do I accept mortality?
- Does wisdom come with aging?
- Why are people spiritual?
- Do we become more spiritual as we age?
- Is there value in meditation?
- How do I find 'peace of mind'?

As we pass through middle age and retirement; as we begin to realize that, we too, are approaching old age, we find ourselves asking questions about the meaning of it all. What is life all about? How can I make sense of it? For what purpose am I here? What more is there for me in this life? It's reassuring to learn that we're not alone in this endeavor. These seem to be natural questions for this stage of life.

Millions of persons long for immortality who do not know what to do with themselves on a rainy afternoon.
Susan Ertz

The psychoanalyst Erik Erikson, in the middle part of the twentieth century, described eight stages of life from Infant to Older Adult or maturity. He suggests that in each stage we have tasks to accomplish or learn. The infant, for example, needs to develop a balance between Trust and Mistrust. Each stage builds on the preceding stages until you reach the Older Adult stage. This stage begins about the time we retire; when we give up our jobs or careers, the children are gone, and we have more time for ourselves. The task for this final stage, according to Erikson, is to develop ego integrity with a minimum of despair. In doing so, we tend to review our life's accomplishments and prepare for the end of life, or death. How we do this work makes all the difference in our final years.

Attitude is everything. As our bodies begin to fail us, we can develop a greater spirituality and a sense of peace with who we are. We can choose to focus on what we're losing—strength and vitality, health, power, friends through death and disease, and perhaps a decreasing financial security. Depression can result if we focus on what we're giving up or what we're losing. How we choose to focus our attention and our energy is pretty much up to us. We've all known aging people who were pessimistic and unhappy and we've known others who were happy and at peace with themselves and the world. Erikson says that those who develop authenticity and approach death without fear have attained wisdom. We can choose to become more authentic individuals.

Our youth dominated culture, in the United States, does not honor and revere age as have some cultures and at some times in history. Today, the elderly are too often ignored or openly scoffed at. The media and the culture reinforce the notion that only the young can be beautiful, healthy and vital. We even tend to view the elderly as incompetent. As a result we want to be young forever! If we can't *be* young, at the very least we want to *look* young.

You can help change those attitudes by being more vocal about the advantages of age and maturity. And, yes, there are advantages. You can read in other sections of this book about things that you can do to make the most of your years of maturity. Let's examine, here, some ways to internalize the reality of aging and show the world that this is a wonderful time of life!

When we're young, we don't have the time or the experience to genuinely make sense of what our lives mean. We're too busy learning, earning a living and taking care of our children. Now, we have the time and the experience to explore the purpose of life and living. As we accomplish this and come to terms with life, it will be evident to those around us. They'll know it by our contentment and the peace and confidence we exude.

Go slowly, breathe and smile.
Thich Nhat Hahn

You can only perceive real beauty in a person as they get older.
Anouk Aimee
1932–, French Actor

RELIGION VS. SPIRITUALITY

Religion and spirituality are often used interchangeably, but they are not necessarily the same. An individual can be both spiritual and religious, or either one without the other. To be religious is to subscribe to the beliefs and practices of an established religion. A person who is religious may also be spiritual, but not necessarily. To be spiritual is to be attuned to a higher force in the universe. Spirituality is about our existence and our place in the world and in the universe. It helps us understand ourselves and others. Spirituality extends beyond the physical self. As I understand it, to be religious is to adhere to the rules of a particular religion; to be spiritual is to find your connection to God.

To know how to grow old is the master work of wisdom, and one of the most difficult chapters in the great art of living.
Henri Frederic Amiel
1821–1881 Swiss
Philosopher, Poet, Critic

For example, Albert follows church doctrine as diligently as he can. He contributes to causes when asked and volunteers for church activities. He contributes financially to support his church. Although he is close to three of his children, Albert no longer has any contact with his youngest son who chose a life style of which Albert does not approve. He considers himself a good Christian but, he sometimes wonders why God has allowed his life to be unhappy. Albert can be described as religious.

In comparison, Amelia does not attend church, but feels connected to a higher power. She reads and studies spiritual writings. She accepts the frailties of people and loves them in spite of their shortcomings. She frequently takes meals to shut-ins or those in need. Amelia volunteers in her community and baby-sits for her grandchildren. She thanks God every day for all of her blessings. Amelia is said to be spiritual.

How beautifully leaves grow old. How full of light and color are their last days.
John Burroughs
1837–1921, American
Naturalist, Author

Lastly, Aaron attends synagogue regularly and follows the prescribed teachings. He loves his family and spends a great deal of time doing things with them. He reads and reflects on ways to make life better for his family and the world community. He strives to strengthen his connection to God. Aaron is both religious and spiritual.

RESEARCH AND SPIRITUALITY

An increasing amount of research is being done to examine the relationship between religion or spirituality and well being or longevity. The research studies have tended to be conducted using religion as a variable because it is easier to define for research purposes. Spirituality is what happens on the inside and therefore more difficult to quantify for research.

Old age is the reward of a well-spent youth. Instead of its bringing sad and melancholy prospects of decay, it would give us hopes of eternal youth in a better world.

Lydia M. Child
1802–1880, American
Abolitionist, Writer, Editor

Studies indicate that attendance at church or religious services seemed to have some health related benefits. A study by Dr. William Strawbridge and other researchers that was published in the American Journal of Public Health in 1997 indicated that religious practice was related to lower blood pressure, less depression, a greater sense of well being, stronger immune systems and greater longevity. Other studies have reported similar findings. "Religious faith seems to increase the ability of older people to cope with illness, disability, loss, and their own mortality."[32]

Dr. Herbert Benson, of the Mind/Body Medical Institute in Boston, has found, from extensive studies, that a process he calls the Relaxation Response has positive effects on the body. It can lower blood pressure, reverse heart disease, and generally increase levels of health and well-being. As you meditate and maintain an attitude of quiet and peace you can strengthen your connection to a higher power.

This Relaxation Response has four steps:

1. Find a quiet environment.
2. Consciously relax the body's muscles.
3. Focus for 10–20 minutes on something such as a prayer or the word "one."
4. Assume a passive attitude toward any intrusive thoughts. Just let them go and resume focus on your word or prayer.

While this exercise or meditation provides real benefits, Dr. Benson found that when it is combined with the person's personal religious or philosophical convictions, the results are even more helpful. He calls this the Faith Factor and describes it thus:

"Not only did my research—and that of my colleagues—reveal that 25% of people feel more spiritual as the result of the Relaxation Response, but it showed that those same people have fewer medical symptoms than do those who reported no increase in spirituality. It became clear that a person's religious convictions or life philosophy enhanced the average effects of the Relaxation Response in three ways: (1) People who chose an appropriate focus, that which drew upon their deepest philosophic or religious convictions, were more apt to adhere to the Relaxation Response routine, looking forward to it and enjoying it; (2) affirmative beliefs of any kind brought forth remembered wellness, reviving top-down, nerve-cell-firing patterns in the brain that were associated with wellness; (3) when present, faith in an eternal or life-transcending force seemed to make the fullest use of remembered wellness because it is a supremely soothing belief, disconnecting unhealthy logic and worries.[16]

This Faith Factor contains two very powerful aspects: prayer or meditation and a deeply held set of religious or philosophical beliefs. Dr. Benson suggests some principles or practical lessons that he's learned from his years of work in this field:

1. Let faith, or the ultimate belief, heal you. A belief in God is good for you.
2. Religious activity is good for you.
3. Trust your instincts more often. Most people have an internal radar that sometimes calls out to them. Ask, "What feels like the right thing to do?" Then follow up your instincts with research, but allow them to be a part of the consideration in decision making.
4. Practice and use self-care on a regular basis. Self-care is whatever you do, on your own, to take care of yourself. This includes good nutrition, exercise, and other things you do to promote your own well-being. Work with your doctor, but remember how important your own care is. Make taking care of yourself a part of what you do—routine.
5. Don't become obsessed with your health and avoidance of aging and dying. Remember that aging and death are natural aspects of living. You can live a fuller and more

If wrinkles must be written upon our brows, let them not be written upon the heart. The spirit should never grow old.
James A. Garfield
1831–1881, 20th President of the USA

From the middle of life onward, only he remains vitally alive who is ready to die with life.
Carl Jung
1875–1961, Swiss Psychiatrist

satisfying life once you accept the inevitable and learn to enjoy every additional day. Live it with passion rather than fear.

6. Beware of people with all the answers. The "gurus," who claim that if you just follow their programs or buy their products, are to be avoided. They don't have all the answers. You have many of the answers in your own inner wisdom if you just tap into it.

7. Believe in something good. You may not need all the pills and procedures that are prescribed, but if you believe they will help it's more probable that they will. Sometimes, you just need a catalyst to stimulate your belief that there will be a good outcome. Remember wellness. Remember what it was like to be completely healthy and full of vigor. Picture yourself feeling like that again.[16]

Age is not all decay; it is the ripening, the swelling, of the fresh life within, that withers and bursts the husk.
George Macdonald
1824–1905, Scottish
Novelist

Others have suggested additional ways to grow spiritually.

1. Join a prayer group that may, or may not, be associated with a religious organization.

2. Meditate regularly for at least twenty minutes and work up to longer periods. It is okay to start with shorter time periods if you're having too much difficulty with twenty minutes.

3. Write your autobiography. What was important about your life? What were the important events that helped shape who you are? Use this task to help you reflect on your life and its meaning. There is meaning, a purpose, for everyone's life.

4. Seek ways to give back to your community. What kind of volunteer work is needed where you live? What would you feel good about contributing?

5. Put together a photograph album that depicts your life. You might use this in conjunction with your autobiography.

The more sand has escaped from the hourglass of our life, the clearer we should see through it.
Jean Paul

6. Compile the family genealogy or write a family history.

7. Tape your memoirs—either audio or video.

8. Use an art medium to express yourself. You might choose sculpture, oil painting, drawing, or any of the other visual media, or you might prefer music. (Grandma Moses started painting when she was in her seventies.)

9. Live in the present moment. The present is, after all, the only time that you have. The past is over and the future hasn't yet arrived. The present moment is the only time in which you can truly be happy.

10. Understand and accept who you are. You are the product of all your life experiences. You can't change the past. Everyone has both strengths and weaknesses. Accept them. Now is the time to realize that you're not perfect and it's perfectly okay to be imperfect.

11. Love. Increase the love in your life. This isn't romantic love, although that's good, too. This is love in the generic sense. Pay attention to those you love and expand that love to more people. Make peace with anyone in your life with whom you are not at peace. Practice unconditional love—love that doesn't require anything in return.

Age should not have its face lifted, but it should rather teach the world to admire wrinkles as the etchings of experience and the firm line of character.
Ralph B. Perry

As you venture into any of these activities, you will want to reflect about your life. What has it been like? What have you learned? What was most important to you when you were younger? What is most important to you now? Has what's important to you changed over the span of your life?

It is important to ask yourself if you believe that the only goal of spirituality in aging is to maintain health. Many people, and I agree with them, think it is not. Hindu tradition encourages older adults to seek spiritual enlightenment. It is the goal of Native American cultures to know themselves and to help others. They encourage their aging members to use their accumulated wisdom and experience to advise the tribe. Spiritual enlightenment combined with the wisdom that can be achieved in old age can make for powerful mentoring of the young. What a wonderful way to leave a legacy to the world.

As Winter strips the leaves from around us, so that we may see the distant regions they formerly concealed, so old age takes away our enjoyments only to enlarge the prospect of the coming eternity.
Jean Paul Richter
1763–1825, German Novelist

THE TASKS OF AGING

Aging and dying are natural aspects of living, and we must make sense of them as part of the life process. Carl Jung, the noted Swiss psychiatrist, spoke about this natural progression from birth to death. He noted the futility of fighting against what is natural and cannot be changed.

Fighting against what we can't change creates fear. If we give purpose to the earlier stages of life, why then do we think the end of life is meaningless? The decline should hold as much purpose as the ascent. The Rev. Ms. Sue E. Sinnamon, in her article "Spirituality and Aging", cites the seven tasks of aging as suggested by the Jungians.[125]

Like a morning dream, life becomes more and more bright the longer we live, and the reason of everything appears more clear. What has puzzled us before seems less mysterious, and the crooked paths look straighter as we approach the end.
Jean Paul Richter
1763–1825, German
Novelist

1. **To face the reality of age and death.** We can only live life fully if we accept the reality of death.
2. **To review, reflect upon, and sum up one's life.** We need to tell our stories; share something of ourselves with others.
3. **Set boundaries about how we expend our time and energy.** When we realize that we have a limited amount of time remaining, it becomes more important to use our time and energy well. We stop doing those things that we determine are a waste of our time.
4. **Let go of ego dominance.** Realize that things don't have to go the way we want them to. Let go of the need to control.
5. **Integrate all the aspects of who we are.** We are made up of numerous opposites; good and bad, honesty and dishonesty, love and hate. We need to understand that the good cannot exist in isolation and integrate all aspects of ourselves.
6. **Find the meaning in our lives.** How did my life fit into the world in which I've been living? What is the purpose or meaning of my life?
7. **Rebirth.** Live life creatively and playfully. Living itself becomes the point. Explore all the possibilities that life has to offer.

You might look at these steps as a progression from the hard cold face of reality to the letting go of concern and into creativity and playfulness. This nudges us into the belief that life does have meaning and purpose, therefore you can let go of worries and concerns and just be who you are.

"Fear of death is like fear of living, we can see it and greet it as a friend, or we can let the fear block our ability to live fully. A living death. Jung says to let living itself become the point. We will all get to face the prison of old age and face our fears of death. We can choose to do it with meaning in our community or we can strive for eternal youth. Becoming who we are is the task life sets before us. We are on the continuum from birth to death. We can cling, drag, strive, shout, and claw against what is our natural cycle, or we can see the richness in the last twenty years of life that is as profound as the years before. We can pray and sing and tell old tales and laugh. We can live with faith and grace."[125]

BRAIN SCIENCE AND THE BIOLOGY OF BELIEF

No wise man ever wished to be younger.
Jonathan Swift 1667–1745, Anglo-Irish Satirist

If you have a curious mind and are especially interested in the basis for spirituality, you might want to look closer at a book on this topic, *Why God Won't Go Away: Brain Science and the Biology of Belief* by Andrew Newberg and Eugene D'Aquili. The authors are medical doctors, professors and brain researchers. In this book, they examine why human beings through the ages and in every culture have been interested in God and spirituality. The authors suggest that the religious impulse has its roots in the human brain; that there is a portion of the brain geared for the religious experience. What they report is far more complex than can be treated here intelligently, but essentially says that the human brain is programmed for the spiritual experience or connection to a higher power in the universe. God won't go away because "God" is hardwired into the human brain.

SPIRITUAL ACTIVITY

Materials: paper and pencil or pen
Directions: Write a letter to God. Tell God your thoughts and feelings. Answer these questions or others that are important to you.

- What are you grateful for?
- What do you worry about?
- Who do you want God to watch over?
- What do you want help with?
- What do you need guidance about?
- What else are you grateful for?

Maturity is the ability to think, speak and act your feelings within the bounds of dignity. The measure of your maturity is how spiritual you become during the midst of your frustrations.
Source Unknown

In such journeys, time is our ally, not our enemy. We can grow wise. As the arteries harden, the spirit can lighten. As the legs fail, the soul can take wing. Things do add up. Life does have shape and maybe even purpose. Or so it seems to me.
Sylvia Fraser

Write letters to God regularly. You may want to keep them in a notebook or a journal. Sometimes it's helpful to look back at what you've written in the past.

CONCLUSION

Spirituality is about the internal recognition that we are not alone in life or in the universe. There is a higher power. Life does have meaning and purpose. We're here for a reason. As we age, we feel a greater need to connect with this higher power and find the meaning in our lives. We strive to give up the less meaningful aspects of life and bring greater focus to what is truly important. We strive to attain wisdom, not just knowledge or power. We strive to achieve inner peace and project that peace into the world.

NOTES FOR PLANNING TO MAXIMIZE MY LIFE SPIRITUALLY

CHAPTER 5

SOCIAL ENGAGEMENT WITH LIFE

- What can I do about loneliness?
- How important are social contacts?
- Does my attitude affect how I age?
- What can I do about depression?
- How can I maintain a positive attitude?
- What can I do to look younger?
- What activities can I get involved in?
- How can I get information about volunteering?

We've always known that people who have lots of friends or big families seem to be happier than those who don't. People who are actively engaged with others just don't seem to get depressed or lonely. What we've learned more recently is that people with large or strong social support networks are healthier and live longer.

Some people who are seemingly quite healthy die in their 60s while others who are physically and medically frail live into their 80s and 90s. Thomas Glass, assistant professor at Harvard, reported on a study reviewing this phenomenon. He and colleagues found that **social activities seemed to be as good as exercise for health and longevity**.

What do we live for, if it is not to make life less difficult for each other?
George Eliot

Loneliness and isolation are among the most common concerns for individuals as they get older. Their children move away and they begin to lose friends, and even spouses, to death. **Loneliness may be harder to endure than sadness, fatigue, anxiety, or memory problems.** Unless a conscious effort is made to remain socially involved, a person might find themselves sitting at home alone.

TIPS FOR INCREASING
SOCIAL CONTACT

Fortunately, there are many things you can do to maintain and build social relationships and contacts.

1. **Maintain and enhance a positive attitude.** This will go a long way in increasing social contact. It's more pleasant to be around someone who is positive and cheerful.
2. **Maintain and enhance your sense of humor.** Laughing is good for you and stimulates good relationships.
3. **Invite someone to lunch**—either in your home or in a restaurant.
4. **Call your sister/brother/a friend** just to say hello.
5. **Join community organizations.** This will get you involved with a group of people on a regular basis.
6. **Join a religious group.** These provide a multitude of opportunities to interact with others in a variety of ways.
7. **Go on a trip** with your spouse, a friend, or a group.
8. **Take a class** in something that interests you. You can do this at the local community college, the local school district community education program, or other places in your community. Check the local newspaper, the yellow pages, ask a neighbor or look in the mail for community education flyers.
9. **Get a part-time job.** Earn some money for using your skills and talents and meet some new people in the process. You can do something on a part time basis that interests you, but you couldn't do when you were younger because it wouldn't support you and your family.
10. **Volunteer your time** doing something that is of particular interest to you. Volunteerism is an outstanding way to meet new people and to gain a sense of making a contribution.
11. **Start a neighborhood bridge (or some other card game) group.** Or this could be walking, or crafts, or anything that interests you and others in your neighborhood. It could be gourmet cooking, monthly dinner gatherings in a local restaurant—the possibilities are endless.

I figured out the only reason to be alive is to enjoy it!
Rita Mae Brown

An archaeologist is the best husband a woman can have; the older she gets the more interested he is in her.
Agatha Christie
1891–1976, British
Mystery Writer

12. **Spend more time with your grandchildren.** Take them on a trip. Invite them to spend the weekend with you. Grandchildren will lift your spirits better than anyone else can. This is good for your grandchildren, as well as for you. It will give them enduring lifetime memories of grandma or grandpa.

13. **Do something silly.** It's good to be able to laugh at yourself. We tend to take ourselves too seriously. Life should be fun.

14. **Do errands for a sick friend.** It will be good for you as well as your friend.

15. Make a special effort to **keep in contact with young people**. This will help you maintain some continuity with issues of concern when you were younger, such as work, child care, and the quality of schools. It will expand your thinking and help you see the world through the eyes of others who are younger.

16. **Build up your tolerance for being alone.** As you get older, it is likely that you will spend more time alone. Being alone gives you time for reading, reflection, writing, hobbies, or whatever you enjoy that doesn't require interaction with someone else.

17. **Get a pet**, especially if you live alone. Pets provide many of the same benefits as human relationships.

18. **Work in the garden.** Interaction with living things of any kind provides benefits.

Research is reinforcing the idea that social involvement and longer healthier lives are related. Perhaps the most noteworthy is the MacArthur Foundation Study reported by John W. Rowe, M.D. and Robert L. Kahn, Ph.D. in their book, *Successful Aging*.[113]

They cite four findings regarding social interaction and health:

1. Isolation is a serious risk factor for your health.
2. Social support can lessen some of the health-related effects of aging.
3. Social support has a positive impact on health and can come in two forms:
   a. Emotional support
   b. Physical assistance

Those who love deeply never grow old; they may die of old age, but they die young.
Benjamin Franklin 1706–1790, American Scientist, Publisher, Diplomat

It is only necessary to grow old to become more charitable and even indulgent. I see no fault committed by others that I have not committed myself.
Johann Wolfgang VonGoethe 1749–1832, German Poet, Dramatist, Novelist

4. No single kind of social support is right for every-one.[113]

For example, Edith, aged 83, was having trouble with her vision and was diagnosed with macular degeneration. Her daughter, trying to be helpful, began doing more things for her mother—taking her meals, cleaning her house. Edith began to believe that she couldn't do things for her-self anymore. She began to depend on her daughter to do more and more things for her—select her clothing, pay her bills, and drive her to appointments. Edith was not learn-ing to make the adaptations that were necessary to main-tain her independence as her sight diminished. She began to become more depressed as she focused on what she couldn't do. Fortunately, her daughter realized what was happening and got her mother enrolled in a workshop that taught her how to do many routine tasks with low vision. Edith is residing in an assisted living facility, interacting with others, and generally enjoying life as she copes with her difficulties.

This example illustrates how too much physical assis-tance can interfere with well-being. Edith's daughter want-ed to help because she cared about her mother, but she, initially, provided more support than was optimal for Edith. We all need emotional support and we may need physical assistance at some time in our lives. The trick is to strike a balance between the support we provide and the support that's needed. We need to be our own best advo-cates in getting the kind of support that we need.

Connie, who was 65 when her husband died, gives us an example of the importance of self advocacy and social support. Suddenly, after the death of her husband, it was necessary for her to became more independent. She lived alone, and felt alone, for the first time in her life. She kept busy cooking, cleaning, shopping, and taking care of the chores her husband had previously done. She took trips with friends. In addition, she cared for her two grandsons while their mother worked. This helped her feel needed, it kept her involved with others every day, and she received

The older woman's love is not love of herself, nor of herself mirrored in a lover's eyes, nor is it corrupted by need. It is a feeling of tenderness so still and deep and warm that it gilds every grass blade and blesses every fly. It includes the ones who have a claim on it, and a great deal else besides. I wouldn't have missed it for the world.
Germaine Greer
1939–, Australian Feminist Writer

regular positive feedback and affection. She intuitively knew what she needed to assuage her loneliness and she did it.

Rowe and Kahn, in *Successful Aging*, report on six different kinds of support activities:[113]

1. confiding
2. reassuring
3. providing sick care
4. expressing respect
5. expressing affection
6. talking about health problems

The quality, not the longevity, of one's life is what is important.
Martin Luther King
1929–1968, American
Black Leader, Nobel Prize
Winner

It is important to have someone in your support network who can provide each of those types of support. Think about your friends, relatives, and colleagues and identify someone who can provide each of those supports for you. Ideally, you will have more than one person in each category, but a single person might provide several kinds of support.

Walter, at 72, had a very close and supportive relationship with his wife of 48 years. They had been through a lot together in life as they raised their four children. When Marie died, Walter was at a loss. Marie was the one in whom he had confided and who reassured him. They had supported each other in virtually every way, but now without her he was truly at a loss. He felt that he had been abandoned. Walter was lonely and depressed. He finally, almost in desperation, confided in a couple of his golf buddies, and when he did he learned an important lesson. His friends did understand and could offer him some reassurance. Over time, Walter was able to fill in all the supports that he needed.

What Walter went through is a common experience among the elderly. He had to realign his social support system due to the loss of someone very close to him. It's important to recognize that you're not alone when confronted with such a crisis. Look around you and extend yourself to others. Begin to strengthen those connections while life is secure. Also consider to whom you might be supportive.

COSMETICS AND AGING

Often it is the social interaction that causes you to feel old. You begin to notice that younger people around you begin to think of you as old, even though you still feel decades younger than your chronological years. This has led to a booming business in the cosmetics industry and in related fields. These are some of the primary things available to alter the appearance of aging:

For age is opportunity no less than youth itself, though in another dress, and as the evening twilight fades away, the sky is filled with stars, invisible by day.
Henry Wadsworth Longfellow
1819–1892, American Poet

- Cosmetic creams and lotions sometimes make outrageous claims regarding their effectiveness in reversing the signs of aging. The research indicates that these may offer some improvement to fine lines and slight signs of aging, but do not provide dramatic results. Prices vary widely and expensive does not necessarily mean better.
- Cosmetic or plastic surgery is available to alter most any aspect of your appearance.
  - A face lift (rhytidoplasty) removes the sags and wrinkles from the lower portion of the face and neck. Incisions are made behind the hairline at the temple, in front of the ear, around the earlobe and behind the ear. The skin is tightened and excess skin removed.
  - A forehead lift requires small incisions above the hairline and the skin is tightened to remove the wrinkles on the forehead.
  - Eyelid surgery (blepharoplasty) is performed on either the upper lids, lower lids or both. Incisions are made in a crease of the upper lids or just below the lower lashes and excess skin is removed.
  - Skin rejuvenation includes laser resurfacing, chemical peels and sanding (dermabrasion). These procedures are used to improve the appearance of the skin and to remove small wrinkles, and irregular pigmentation.
  - Botox injections involve the use of small needles to place botulinum toxin type A into the muscle around facial lines, especially "crow's feet" and forehead lines. Botox relaxes the muscle or "freezes" it so the wrinkles disappear. The effects are temporary, usually lasting for several months.
- Hair transplants are used to reduce the appearance of

baldness, usually in men. These are complicated and time consuming procedures which may require numerous visits over a year or two. Several methods are used.

- ○ Hair grafting involves the removal of small sections of hair from the sides or back of the head and moving them to the top of the scalp.
- ○ In flap surgery a larger section of hair is partially detached and used to cover the balding area. A portion remains attached to the original site.
- ○ Scalp reduction is the removal of a section of the balding scalp. This procedure is typically used with hair grafting.
- ○ With scalp expansion, silicone bags are inserted underneath the skin to enlarge a section of hair-bearing scalp. This procedure is often used with flap surgery and the expanded section of scalp is extended to cover an area of baldness.

- Anti-aging medicine is a growing field in which a doctor will prescribe products and activities to suit your individual needs. The doctor first performs blood and other appropriate tests to determine your specific deficiencies and then prescribes an anti-aging regimen for you. Often this regimen includes human growth hormone (HGH), DHEA, estrogen, testosterone, and/or other supplements for your specific needs. While it is not strictly speaking cosmetic, it seems to fall within the same conversation since some of the benefits are purported to be cosmetic.

- Teeth bleaching or whitening can make your smile look more youthful. Your teeth tend to yellow and stain as you get older dulling your smile. A dentist will make a pliable tray for you that conforms to your teeth and sell you the bleaching solution. Once you've whitened your teeth to the desired shade, you'll need to do a touch up every few weeks.

The question of what to do, if anything, in an effort to look younger is an individual choice. There are strongly held opinions on both sides of the question and arguments to support them. In the end, you will decide for yourself what is best for you. Remember that's one of the best advantages of getting older—you can do what you want to do regardless of the opinions of others.

When we are out of sympathy with the young, then I think our work in this world is over.
George MacDonald
1824–1905, Scottish Novelist

Age does not protect you from love but love to some extent protects you from age.
Jeanne Moreau
1928–, French Actress and Director

VOLUNTEERING

When you're 50 you start thinking about things you haven't thought about before. I used to think getting old was about vanity—but actually it's about losing people you love. Getting wrinkles is trivial.

Joyce Carol Oates
1938–, American Author

Social supports, volunteering and work that entails interaction with others all seem to lead to greater health as we age, according to research studies. These benefits were enjoyed by those with chronic conditions as well as those who exhibited relatively good health. This is good news because it allows for everyone to find a good fit with their own personal interests and preferences. If you don't have a strong network of friends and family, you can find a volunteer activity or part-time job that suits your time available and your skills and talents.

For example, researchers at the University of Michigan found that mature adults who volunteered for a total of less than forty hours during the previous year were less likely to die over the next 7 1/2 years than those who didn't volunteer at all. Interestingly, increasing the amount of volunteer time did not increase the benefit. There may even be a detrimental effect to taking on too much volunteer activity. Apparently, you can have too much of a good thing, and then it's no longer a good thing. Marc A. Musick, the lead author of the study, and his colleagues found the greatest benefits of volunteering were for men and women with little social interaction otherwise. You are the best judge of the amount of volunteerism that is optimal for you.

It is theorized that one reason for the health benefits of volunteering may be that it provides purpose and meaning in one's life. If you remember the work of Victor Frankel, author of *Man's Search for Meaning*, you know how important it is to have some purpose or meaning in your life. Frankel was a psychiatrist who survived the Nazi concentration camps of WWII and went on to make use of his experiences. He speculated that those who survived the concentration camps were those who believed they had strong reasons for doing so. They had some purpose in life that caused them to believe their survival would mean something to those they loved and to the world. Volunteering may help seniors find some reason to keep living. You can make a contribution; you *can* make a difference whatever your age.

Volunteer efforts provide valuable services in uncountable ways. Volunteers help sick or disabled people get hot meals on a regular basis. They provide comfort to sick children. They help the illiterate learn to read. They assist in cleaning up the environment. They take care of lost pets at the humane society. The list of contributions of volunteers is endless. Efforts to quantify the contributions of senior volunteers in hours and in dollars and cents have estimated that volunteers donate many thousands of hours and millions of dollars to the economy each year. Literally, our way of life is improved because so many retired people are willing to contribute their time, energy, skills, talents, expertise, and labor to scores of projects they deem worthwhile. It is fitting that they should derive some benefit in greater longevity.

When senior volunteers were asked about their experiences they cited these benefits:[5]

An old man loved is winter with flowers.
German Proverb

1. meeting new people
2. gaining new experiences
3. finding new challenges
4. feeling good and increasing self-esteem
5. fulfilling the need to be needed
6. pride in sharing skills and abilities
7. keeping the mind active
8. keeping the body active
9. staying healthy
10. having fun
11. greater self-confidence
12. improved immune system functioning
13. lower blood pressure
14. greater mental alertness
15. more vitality and longevity

This is an impressive list of positives to be derived from donating one's time, energy, and skills.

Bob's story is a good one to illustrate the importance of selecting a volunteer activity wisely. He had worked at a desk job for most of his adult life, and on weekends he enjoyed working in the garden and doing things outside. After he retired, Bob devoted more of his time to the local service club. He became treasurer and did other organizational maintenance kinds of activities, but he was not really happy with them. He got restless. Then the club started an environmental project, planting trees at various places in the community. Bob found his niche. Working outside on environmental projects was what he found he really wanted to do.

It is important to remember that if you are going to be a volunteer, you need to find something that suits you, something that you will enjoy doing. There's no personal benefit in volunteering if it isn't rewarding to you in some way. Consider these questions:

No one grows old by living. Only by losing interest in living.
Marie Beyon Ray

1. What do you like to do in your free time?
2. How much activity are you comfortable with? A little or a lot?
3. How much time do you want to contribute?
4. Do you want/need a flexible schedule or a fixed schedule?
5. Do you have transportation to get to/from your volunteer position? If not, what are the options?
6. What volunteer positions are available in your community? Or elsewhere, if you want to travel?
7. What skills, talents, special interests do you want to share?
8. Do you like to work with children? Adolescents? Adults? Seniors? The handicapped?
9. Do you like to work with nature? The environment? Animals?
10. Do you want to work outside? Inside?

With mirth and laughter let old wrinkles come.
[Merchant of Venice]
William Shakespeare

There are possibilities available for virtually any set of descriptors that you can identify. The trick is to get a good match between what you want and what is needed. If you need a place to start your search for the perfect match for you, try one, or more, of these websites.

- The Corporation for National Service, www.national service.org. This organization was created by Congress with bipartisan support. The website provides news and opportunities for volunteering in your community. You can search by zip code and by the type of service you would like to provide. It is an excellent resource. Also look at www.nationalservice.org/stateprofiles, for help in identifying volunteer opportunities in your state. There are three initiatives to choose from:

- ○ AmeriCorps
- ○ Learn and Serve America
- ○ National Senior Service Corps

- The Senior Corps, www.seniorcorps.org, is operated as a part of the Corporation for National Service. Contact information is provided by state and area. Senior Corps includes three programs:

  - ○ Retired and Senior Volunteer Program (RSVP)
  - ○ Foster Grandparent Program
  - ○ Senior Companion Program

You can also find volunteer opportunities by:

- Calling the local hospitals
- Calling the local school or school district
- Contacting environmental organizations
- Contacting the humane society
- Reading the local newspaper
- Asking friends, family, colleagues
- Checking with your religious organization—church, temple, synagogue, mosque, or other

That man never grows old who keeps a child in his heart.
Sir Richard Steele
1672–1729, British
Dramatist, Essayist, Editor

ACTIVITY FOR SOCIAL ENGAGEMENT

Try this activity to help you examine socialization in your life—what it is and what you'd like it to be.

Materials: unlined paper, pencils or pens in two different colors

Directions:

1. Draw a circle in the middle of your unlined paper and write "desired social interactions" in the circle.
2. Reflect about the kinds of social interaction that you would like to have in your life, such as someone to travel with, someone to confide in, or someone to laugh with, and so on. As you think of a category draw a circle, write it in the circle, and draw a line connecting it to the center circle. You can make this diagram as complex as you want.
3. Using a pen of another color, write the names of people

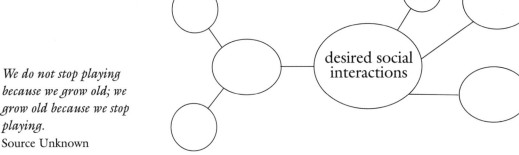

We do not stop playing because we grow old; we grow old because we stop playing.
Source Unknown

in your life with which you exchange the desired kinds of social interaction. Put the names beside the kind of interaction they provide.

4. Take a look at the social supports that you have in your life. Where is it good and where would you like to enhance your socialization? Reflect on what you see in your diagram and what it means to you.

5. Develop a plan for filling in the voids and for maximizing the supports that currently exist. See the "Tips for Increasing Social Contact" above to help you with your plan.

Life without love is a bird without a song. Life without trust is a night without day. Life without faith is a tree without root. Life without hope is a year without Spring. Life without friends is a sun without shade. Life without work is a bloom without fruit.
Dr. William Arthur Ward

CONCLUSION

Social activities and social support networks are essential to the quality of your life, especially as you grow older. Increasing socialization may take the place of some of the more active things you did when you were younger. You have fewer responsibilities for things like full time jobs and the day-to-day care of young children. You have more time to nurture friendships and these friendships become more important to you. They not only bring pleasure, they also contribute to your health and well being and even to your longevity. Be grateful for every friend and nurture every friendship.

NOTES FOR PLANNING TO MAXIMIZE MY LIFE SOCIALLY AND EMOTIONALLY

CHAPTER 6

THE IMPORTANCE OF
FINANCIAL PLANNING

- Am I prepared financially for retirement?
- Should I have a financial planner?
- How can I find a reputable financial planner?
- What questions should I ask to select a good financial planner?
- What kinds of professionals provide financial planning services?
- What credentials does a good financial planner have?
- How can I check their credentials?

The question of financial security in our maturing years is vastly complex and I claim no special knowledge about your money or even my own. Unless you have some skill or expertise, or at least a keen interest combined with a willingness to do the constant research required, you will probably want to work with a financial advisor. What I can do, however, is give you some pointers about what you should know and how to get started in finding a good financial advisor.

Money is better than poverty, if only for financial reasons.
Woody Allen
Comedian

Financial planning is pretty much what it sounds like—the process of identifying your financial status, your goals, and how you will go about meeting them. When doing your financial planning you'll want to think about these questions.

1. When do you plan to retire?
2. How much income will you have from pensions or part time employment?
3. How much will you get from social security?

4. How much can you expect from your investments?
5. What will your expenses be?
6. How will your expenses change when you are retired?
7. Do you want to travel or engage in some other costly activity?
8. How much money will you need?
9. How much will you have?
10. How can you make up the difference?

It is the heart that makes a man rich. He is rich according to what he is, not according to what he has.
Henry Ward Beecher
Writer

If you can answer all those questions on your own you don't need the help of an advisor. If, however, you're like most people, the answers to questions 4 and 10 above (and perhaps several others) are tough to find. The prospect of researching all those stocks, bonds, and mutual funds is more than a bit daunting. If you want to locate a good reputable professional to assist you, don't just pick a name from the yellow pages.

A good financial advisor can help you look at the big picture and answer some of those questions posed above. A professional can help you identify where you are at the present time and identify a strategy to meet your goals. You won't turn over the decisions to someone else, but you can get help in analyzing the relevant information. You will get recommendations, but you will make all the decisions unless you choose to turn that power over to someone else. You will have the expert available to ask questions, to assist you in diversifying your investments, and to examine the short and long term implications of your decisions.

IDENTIFYING A PROFESSIONAL WITH WHOM TO WORK

There are several different professional designations that you will want to understand when looking for an advisor. They have differing kinds of education, training, licensing or certification, and expertise.

Accountant

While accountants work for all major companies, individuals usually seek their assistance for tax related issues such as filling out annual tax forms for the Internal Revenue Service. Accountants who practice as Certified Public Accountants (CPA) must be licensed by the state in which they do business. A CPA may have no special knowledge or expertise regarding investment matters.

Estate Planner

An estate planner can help your heirs manage your assets at the time of death. They provide information on estate taxes and other estate planning issues. Only attorneys can prepare the legal documents that will direct your assets upon your death—documents such as wills, trusts and powers of attorney. Estate planners may hold an Accredited Estate Planner (AEP) designation.

Financial Planner

There are three designations of professional financial planners that you should know about.

1. **Certified Financial Planner (CFP)**—This designation requires the completion of a course of study, passage of a rigorous examination on financial planning, and at least three years of work experience in the financial planning field, as well as other educational and ethical requirements.
2. **Chartered Financial Consultants (ChFC)**—ChFCs must have completed a designated course of study and passed examinations on personal finance offered by the American College in Bryn Mawr, Pennsylvania.
3. **Personal Financial Specialist (CPA-PFS)**—This is a Certified Public Accountant (CPA) who has also been certified as a Personal Finance Specialist. The PFS designation is awarded by the American Institute of CPAs when specified requirements in personal financial planning are met. This is a CPA specialist. Not all CPAs are qualified to help you with financial planning.

I'm not into the money thing. You can only sleep in one bed at a time. You can only eat one meal at a time, or be in one car at a time. So I don't have to have millions of dollars to be happy. All I need are clothes on my back, a decent meal, and a little loving when I feel like it. That's the bottom line.
Ray Charles
Singer

The government does not regulate financial planners as financial planners, consequently anyone can claim to be a financial planner. You will want to check up on the certifications cited above to make sure that you are working with someone who is qualified to work with you on the comprehensive aspects of your planning.

Insurance Agents

Insurance agents are required to be licensed by the state in which they work. Insurance agents may also be Chartered Life Underwriters (CLU). Financial planners may provide advice about insurance, but they cannot sell it to you unless they have been licensed to do so.

Modern man is frantically trying to earn enough to buy things he's too busy to enjoy.
Frank A. Clark

Investment Advisor

An investment advisor is anyone who is paid to provide advice regarding securities and must register with the Securities and Exchange Commission or state securities agencies. They must have a securities license in order to sell securities.

Stockbrokers

Stockbrokers must be licensed to buy and sell securities such as stocks, bonds and mutual funds. They must also be registered with a company that is a member of the National Association of Securities Dealers (NASD) and pass examinations administered by NASD.

When I chased after money, I never had enough. When I got my life on purpose and focused on giving of myself and everything that arrived into my life, then I was prosperous.
Wayne Dyer
Psychotherapist, Author

When engaging in your financial planning make sure that you know what kind of advice you will need and seek out the most appropriate professional. If you need help with your taxes, see a CPA. If you want to buy insurance, see an insurance agent. If you want help with your overall financial planning to meet specific goals, see a financial planner, but if you use a financial planner verify that he/she is qualified to assist you in the way you desire.

SELECTING A FINANCIAL ADVISOR

When selecting a financial advisor, you'll want to get recommendations from friends, family, or colleagues. You should not, however, stop with the recommendations. You'll want to interview a few good prospects to see which

one will work best for you. You may have different preferences and needs than your friends and you'll want to find
the one that is the closest match for what you need.

You'll want to find out about their background and
qualifications. What services do they offer? You'll want to
know whether they specifically provide the services that
you want or need. Ask them to tell you how they will take
you through the planning process. What will it entail? Another important matter is whether you'll work with one
person or several people. How much do they charge and
how do they collect it—through fees, commissions, or
salary? It will be important for you to know if those recommending products and services to you will benefit from
that sale. For example, will they get a commission on an insurance policy that you buy?

The following interview form was adapted from the
one found on the website of the Certified Financial Planner Board of Standards (see Resources in the back of this
book) and will provide you with an excellent guide for determining which professional is best for you. The interview
conversation will also help you decide which one you can
work with most compatibly. Ask everyone the same basic
set of questions so you'll have a better basis for comparison.

Ask in advance whether there will be a charge for this
introductory interview. Most planners will give you a half
hour or an hour for this purpose without charging you.

Money has never made man happy, nor will it, there is nothing in its nature to produce happiness. The more of it one has the more one wants.
Benjamin Franklin

I've always thought anyone can make money. Making a life worth living, that's the real test.
Robert Fulghum
Writer

1. Do you have experience in providing advice on these
    topics? How many years?
    ☐ Retirement planning
    ☐ Investment planning
    ☐ Tax planning
    ☐ Estate planning
    ☐ Insurance planning
    ☐ Integrated planning
    ☐ Other
2. In what areas do you specialize? What has prepared
    you to specialize in that area(s)?
3. Will you provide a written analysis of my financial situ-
    ation and recommendations?

4. Do you provide recommendations for specific investments?

5. Do you assist with implementation of those recommendations?

6. Do you offer continuous, on-going advice regarding my financial affairs? How often will we meet and talk?

7. Will you have access to my assets? Can you buy or sell without my explicit permission?

8. How long have you been offering financial advice to clients?

9. How many clients do you have at this time?

10. What is the range of asset value of your clients? (You want to be sure your assets fall within the range.)

11. Tell me about your work history. (Where have you worked and for how long? What did you do there?)

12. What are your educational qualifications? What was your field of study?
   ☐ Undergraduate degree
   ☐ Post graduate degree
   ☐ Other

13. What financial planning designations do you hold?
   ☐ Certified Financial Planner (CFP)
   ☐ Certified Public Accountant—Personal Financial Specialist (CPA-PFS)
   ☐ Chartered Financial Consultant (ChFC)

14. What continuing education do you pursue in the field of financial planning?

15. What licenses do you hold?
   ☐ Insurance
   ☐ Securities
   ☐ CPA
   ☐ JD
   ☐ Other

16. If you have a license to sell securities, are you registered with the:
   ☐ State
   ☐ Federal government
   ☐ If no, why not?

17. Is your firm licensed or registered as an Investment Advisor with the:
   ☐ State
   ☐ Federal government
   ☐ If no, why not?

I need just enough to tide me over until I need more.
Bill Hoest

It's good to have money and the things that money can buy, but it's good, too, to check up once in a while and make sure you haven't lost the things that money can't buy.
George Horace Latimer

18. If you sell securities, may I have a copy of your disclosure document Form ADV (if registered with the federal government - SEC) or its state equivalent form?

19. Please describe the process you use for financial planning including the services you offer.

20. Who will work with me on my plan?
    - ☐ CFP
    - ☐ CPA-PFS
    - ☐ ChFC
    - ☐ An associate

21. Will the same person review my financial situation?

22. How are you paid for your services?
    - ☐ Fee
    - ☐ Commission
    - ☐ Fee and commission
    - ☐ Salary
    - ☐ Other

23. What do you charge?
    Fee:
    Hourly rate
    Flat fee
    Percentage of assets under management
    Commissions:
    What percentage of the investment (or premium) do you receive on:
    Stocks and bonds
    Mutual funds
    Insurance products
    Other

24. Do you, or your firm, have a business affiliation with a company whose products or services you are recommending? If yes, explain. (Is any of your compensation based on selling products? Do any of the companies or agents to whom you might refer me send business, fees, or any other benefits to you?)

25. Do you own, or are you connected with, any other company whose products or services you might recommend to me?

26. Do you provide a written client engagement agreement? If no, why not?

Be sure that you understand the answers provided to the questions you ask. You should choose an advisor with

I have enough money to last me the rest of my life, unless I buy something.
Jackie Mason
Comedian

The chief value of money lies in the fact that one lives in a world in which it is overestimated.
H.L. Mencken
Author

whom you feel comfortable and this includes fully answering all your questions in a way that makes sense to you. The advisor should be willing to take the time necessary to make sure that the recommendations are clear and understandable to you, and without using unnecessary jargon. They should not rush you regardless of the amount of money you plan to invest. And finally, check them out.

CHECKING CREDENTIALS

Good management is better than good income.
Portuguese Proverb

Unfortunately, you cannot assume that the interview will reveal the whole story. You'll want to check to make sure that they do indeed possess the credentials they said they have and you'll want to know about any disciplinary actions against them. Fortunately, it's a fairly routine matter to check them out. It will just take a little time.

I've listed some places to contact to verify that the persons you're considering working with are qualified in the ways they claim. You can also use these sources to check on past disciplinary actions. Do your homework!

Certified Financial Planner Board of Standards
   1700 Broadsay, Suite 2100
   Denver, CO 80209-2101
   (888)-CFP-MARK
   www.cfp-board.org

North American Securities Administrators Association
   (888)-84-NASSA
   www.nasaa.org/nasaa/abtnasaa/find_regulator.asp
   (to get contact information for state securities regulators)

It is not how much one makes but to what purpose one spends.
John Ruskin
Social Theorist

For a copy of the Form ADV:
Office of Public Reference
450 5th Street, NW, Room 1300
Washington, D.C. 20549-0102
(202)-942-8090
   or to view it online:
   www.adviserinfo.sec.gov/IAPD/Content/IapdMain/
   iapd_SiteMap.asp

National Association of Insurance Commissioners
(816)-842-3600

*I've been rich and I've
been poor. Rich is better.*
Sophie Tucker
Singer

National Association of Securities Dealers
(800)-289-9999
www.nasdr.com/2000.asp

National Fraud Exchange (fee required)
(800)-822-0416

Securities and Exchange Commission
(800)-732-0330
www.sec.gov

WORKING WITH A
FINANCIAL ADVISOR

Once you've selected a financial advisor to work with, you
can expect that he/she will ask you many questions that
will help clarify your current financial situation and your financial goals. In order to gain that information you may be
asked the following kinds of questions.

1. What are your goals? Long term and short term?
2. At what age do you expect to retire?
3. What do you anticipate your annual income will need
   to be when you retire? Will you have a pension?
4. What assets do you have? You will be asked to list all
   your assets -savings, investments, house, car, possessions.
5. What liabilities do you have? What bills do you owe—
   house, car, credit cards, other?
6. How many dependents do you have? Do any of your
   dependents have conditions that might require extra financial expenditures?
7. Do you anticipate any large expenses in the future?
8. How involved do you want to be in making investment
   decisions? Be *very* careful about giving your advisor too
   much control over your money.
9. How great is your tolerance for risk? Do you want your
   money to be invested very conservatively or do you

*I am opposed to
millionaires, but it would
be dangerous to offer me
the position.*
Mark Twain

have a higher tolerance for risk? Typically the more conservative your investments, the lower the rate of return and the safer your money is. The rate of return is greater on more aggressive investments, but you are also more likely to lose money.

Always remember that it is your money and that you have the right to control it. You should always know where your money is and how you can gain access to it. You should also remember that if you decide to withdraw money from a tax sheltered account, you will be required to pay taxes on it and will also be charged a fee if you are less than 59 1/2 years of age.

I've got all the money I'll ever need, if I die by four o'clock.
Henny Youngman
Comedian

Plan to meet with your advisor at least once a year to review your financial goals, plans, and status. Major events in your life can cause changes that will affect your goals or plans. For example, when you do retire you may want to change the way you invest your funds and you may want to start withdrawing from your investments. Your financial advisor can help you make those changes.

SUGGESTIONS FOR STRETCHING YOUR MONEY

Whether you have a lot of money or a little, you will be wise to spend it carefully. Consider the following questions when you plan to make a purchase:

Money won't make you happy . . . but everybody wants to find out for themselves.
Zig Zigler
Motivational Speaker

- Do I need this?
- Can I afford this?
- Will it improve my life?
- Will it make me happier or healthier?
- Is this the best way to use this money?

If you're like me, you could probably answer these questions with a no for a significant percentage of the purchases you make. Sometimes I just want it. Perhaps it will boost my ego for a short while. Maybe it's the latest fashion. It could be that I think it will impress someone or increase my status. How about all those cosmetics that are supposed to make you look younger? They're expensive and most don't work; those that do work don't necessarily make a significant difference.

I've found that my best course is to stay out of stores unless there is something specific that I need. Go in, buy what you need, and leave. Browsing leads to impulse buying—why else would you browse?

If shopping is a recreational activity for you, consider something else to do with your time that doesn't cost so much. How about reading a library book, going for a walk or a bicycle ride. Call or visit a friend. Make a list of all the things you can do for free.

Be not penny-wise. Riches have wings. Sometimes they fly away of themselves, and sometimes they must be set flying to bring in more.
Francis Bacon British Philosopher

Take advantage of senior discounts. Remember to ask if there is a reduced price for senior citizens. There are discounts for services and products ranging from movie theaters, to restaurants, hotels, airfare, museums and many more. If you don't see a sign, ask.

It's a tricky business knowing how much money you have to spend. Unless you're still working, you probably have a fixed income and you don't know how long it has to last. Of course, you know that already. The trick is to balance your spending so that you don't deprive yourself unnecessarily, while stretching your dollars so you don't run out.

Your financial advisor can help you project out over time, but ultimately you have to decide what to buy and what to pass up. Do it as thoughtfully as you can.

Notes for Planning to Maximize My Life Financially

CHAPTER 7

YOUR SENSE OF HUMOR

- Does research tell us anything about humor?
- What benefit does humor provide?
- How can I get more humor in my life?

It feels good to laugh. Intuitively you know that it is good to have a sense of humor. But, is there any value to laughter other than feeling good? Yes. Research is beginning to show the health benefits of a good laugh or an outlook on life that allows you to see the humorous side of a stressful situation.

Humor is defined as a comic, absurd, or incongruous quality causing amusement; or as the faculty of perceiving and expressing or appreciating what is amusing or comical. A sense of humor is a way of perceiving the world that allows us to laugh when we might otherwise cry, or at least, feel considerable stress. Humor makes life more enjoyable.

Humor is just another defense against the universe.
Mel Brooks

We laugh when we are surprised or when what we expect to happen, doesn't. The punch line of a joke is funny because we don't expect it—it catches us off guard.

Research studies are beginning to show that laughing is good for your health. It helps you relax. It lightens your spirits. It offers a valuable perspective on the world. It lessens your anxieties and fears. It bonds people together. Laughter is what makes us human. Animals don't laugh. Humor allows you to create a distance between yourself and your problems and to view them in a new way.

The author, Norman Cousins, made us aware of the physiological benefits of laughter in his book *Anatomy of an Illness*. He used tapes of old comedic movies and performances to relieve himself of the pain and suffering of a crippling arthritic condition. He claimed that ten minutes of hearty laughter (a good belly laugh) allowed him to get two hours of pain free sleep.

Studies on humor have shown it to lower pain thresholds, reduce stress and to boost the immune system. Relaxation exercises also produce positive benefits, but laughing is more spontaneous and more fun.[128]

WARNING: Humor may be hazardous to your illness.
Ellie Katz

Babies begin laughing when they are about ten weeks old. By four months, they are laughing about once an hour. Four-year-olds laugh about every four minutes, but the average adult laughs only about fifteen times per day. We tend to think that we must be serious and responsible and that laughter is frivolous or silly—that it isn't mature behavior. However, adults who go against that trend reap benefits for their rebellious behavior—laughing.

The evidence is increasing that your thoughts, moods, emotions, and belief system affect your basic health and healing mechanisms in fundamental ways. Your healing systems respond well to positive emotions and attitudes. Similarly, you respond poorly to negative emotions and attitudes. Love, hope, optimism, caring, intimacy, joy, laughter and humor make you healthier. Hate, hopelessness, pessimism, indifference, anxiety, depression and loneliness detract from your well being.[90]

A person who knows how to laugh at himself will never cease to be amused.
Shirley Maclaine

Your emotions are stored in the brain as chemicals. Emotions trigger the release of neurotransmitters from neurons in the brain. Neurotransmitters allow all the cells in your body to communicate with each other. They enter the body and travel to receptor sites on the surface of immune cells. These messages tell your body whether it should be sick or well. Positive emotions send wellness messages; negative emotions send illness messages.

Laughter affects the body in the following ways:

- Relaxes the muscles
- Reduces stress hormones
- Enhances the immune system
- Increases immunoglobulins that protect you from colds or flu
- Enhances cellular immunity

- Reduces pain
- Exercises the heart
- May trigger the release of endorphins
- May lower blood pressure
- Produces a general sense of well being

These contribute to greater health for people who build humor into their lives and laugh regularly.

"All this research, done in the past ten years, helps us understand the mind-body connections. The emotions and moods we experience directly effect our immune system. A sense of humor allows us to perceive and appreciate the incongruities of life and provides moments of joy and delight. These positive emotions can create neurochemical changes that will buffer the immunosuppressive effects of stress. Laughter can provide a cathartic release, a purifying of emotions and release of emotional tension. Laughter, crying, raging, and trembling are all cathartic activities which can unblock energy flow."[156]

Comedy is a tragedy plus time.
Carol Burnett

The perception of humor involves the whole brain and integrates and balances the activity between the two hemispheres. The left hemisphere of the cortex analyzes the set-up of the joke as it processes the words. The frontal lobe which is the center of emotionality is also involved. The right hemisphere uses its synthesis capabilities to join with left's processing to find the pattern so it can 'get the joke'. The sensory processing areas of the occipital lobe are then utilized. There is then an increase in fluctuation in delta waves as the brain 'gets' the joke before the external laughter begins.[156]

Humor is a good stimulant for the brain. It requires that the brain be fully involved in the activity.

SUGGESTIONS FOR GETTING MORE LAUGHTER INTO YOUR LIFE

1. Read the comics and cartoons in the newspaper.
2. Watch funny programs on television.
3. Get joke books from the library and read them.
4. Browse through the humor section at a bookstore.

Good humor is a tonic for mind and body. It is the best antidote for anxiety and depression. It is a business asset. It attracts and keeps friends. It lightens human burdens. It is the direct route to serenity and contentment.
Grenville Kleiser

Humor is by far the most significant activity of the human brain.
Edward De Bono

5. Collect jokes from your friends.
6. Tell jokes, even if you don't do it well. You'll get better with practice. If you can laugh at yourself, it might even be funnier to tell it badly.
7. Explore humor sites on the web.
8. Post your favorite cartoons on the refrigerator.
9. Go to humorous movies.
10. Act silly. Do something that you don't usually do, just for fun.
11. Roll down a hill on a sunny afternoon. (This may not be for everyone, but then what is.)
12. Tell jokes with your grandchildren.
13. Laugh when other people tell jokes, even if they're not that funny. Maybe even laugh at how bad they are.
14. Watch for humor in unusual places—in the newspaper or on the radio.
15. Listen to audio tapes of comedians when you're in the car.
16. Play with your grandchildren and laugh with them. Recently, I was playing with my two-year-old granddaughter, Brianna. We were looking for things to view under a magnifying glass. Every time she'd say, "Look at something else, Grandma," I'd say, "Hummmm," as I was thinking of other things to view. Soon she started to imitate me, "Hummmm." We both started giggling and laughing. Now, I know that's no big deal of an event, but that's the point. The best laughs, the most fun, result from the little things that occur all the time.

Humor is a whisper from the soul, imploring mind and body to relax, let go and be at peace again.
Source Unknown

17. Laugh at yourself. It's safe to laugh at ourselves, but not always safe to laugh at others.
18. Laugh at your mistakes. The vast majority of the mistakes we make are not related to the important things of life and probably should be laughed at.
19. Practice looking at the funny side of stressful events— hosting a large family gathering, traveling, painting the house . . . you get the idea. Believe me, there's a lot of humor in these events. It's easier to laugh about the soup boiling over than to stress-out about it.
20. Practice light hearted exaggeration. "Woody Allen once remarked: 'More than any other time in history, humankind faces a crossroads. One path leads to despair and utter hopelessness. The other to total extinc-

tion. Let us pray we have the wisdom to choose correctly.'"[128]

21. Laugh at aging. Jokes and funny stories about aging abound on the web, and everywhere else in our society. If you can exaggerate and laugh about the changes that you're experiencing as you get older, it doesn't seem so bad. It lets you know that you're not alone. Millions of others are sharing your experiences.

This is one of the many humorous pieces on the web about aging:

Comedy is simply a funny way of being serious.
Peter Ustinov

HOW TO KNOW YOU'RE GETTING OLDER

- Everything hurts and what doesn't hurt doesn't work.
- The gleam in your eye is from the sun hitting your bifocals.
- You feel like the morning after and you haven't been anywhere.
- Your little black book contains names only ending in M.D.
- Your children begin to look middle aged.
- You finally reach the top of the ladder and find it's leaning against the wrong wall.
- Your mind makes contracts your body can't keep.
- A dripping faucet causes an uncontrollable bladder urge.
- You look forward to a dull evening.
- Your favorite part of the newspaper is "20 Years Ago Today."
- You turn out the light for economic reasons rather than romantic ones.
- You sit in the rocking chair and can't get it going.
- Your knees buckle and your belt won't.
- You regret all those mistakes you made resisting temptations.
- You're 17 around the neck, 42 around the waist, and 96 around the golf course.
- Your back goes out more than you do.
- Your pacemaker makes the garage door open when you see a pretty girl.

Anyone who takes himself too seriously always runs the risk of looking ridiculous; anyone who can consistently laugh at himself does not.
Vaclav Havel

- The little old gray haired lady you help across the street is your wife.
- You sink your teeth into a steak and they stay there.
- You have too much room in the house and not enough in the medicine cabinet.
- You know all the answers but nobody asks the questions.[68]

Humor is the affectionate communication of insight.
Leo Rosten
Political Scientist

ACTIVITY FOR INCREASING HUMOR

Humor Scrapbook

Materials: You can use a scrapbook or any other kind of book you choose as long as it has blank pages. The pages can be lined or unlined. You'll also need scissors and glue.

Directions:

1. Collect jokes, cartoons, comic strips, funny stories—anything that makes you laugh—and put them into your Humor Scrapbook.
2. Write your own funny stories or jokes.
3. Draw funny pictures.
4. Have a grandchild draw a funny picture for you.
5. Put in humorous photographs.
6. You may want to decorate the cover in a pleasing or humorous way.

Good humor isn't a trait of character, it is an art which requires practice.
DavidSeabury
Doctor, Author

The only rule to this activity is that your scrapbook is to include only things that you find humorous. When you need a laugh, bring out your Humor Scrapbook.

CONCLUSION

While I was not able to find research evidence regarding a direct relationship between humor and aging, I believe that the studies showing a correlation between laughter and health have a relationship to the aging process. Aging has long been associated with the deterioration of the body. **If laughter can help us achieve and maintain good health,**

it stands to reason that it can have a positive impact on the aging process.

Humor is a good self care tool. It can provide important health benefits and help us cope with life in an optimistic way. It can help us laugh at our problems. It can help us steer away from depression and foster a positive attitude about living.

The comic and the tragic lie inseparably close, like light and shadow.
Socrates

NOTES FOR PLANNING TO
MAXIMIZE MY LIFE SENSE OF HUMOR

CHAPTER 8

PUTTING IT ALL TOGETHER

For the first time in history people are facing the possibility of living to be 100 years old, or even older. This is a monumental change from past generations. The average life expectancy has increased from 47 in 1900 to more than 76 by 2000. As we continue to find ways to cure diseases and promote health, it is reasonable to expect that number to increase even more. Additionally, scientists are searching for information about the human aging process—what causes it and how to delay it. Longevity, as we know it, continues to be altered upward.

Grow old with me the best is yet to come.
Robert Browning

If 76 is the present life expectancy, it is clear that many people are living well beyond that. There is some evidence to indicate that the sixties are a vulnerable decade for disease. If you live beyond that, you have an increased chance to live a very long life because you were hardy enough to get through this risky period.

It's important for you to decide how long you want to live, because what you do, your life choices, make a difference. If you're not concerned about living a long life, you don't need to do so much planning and preparation. But if you really want to reach 90 or 100, you have to prepare for it—physically, mentally, socially, emotionally, financially and spiritually.

Perhaps one has to be very old before one learns to be amused rather than shocked.
Pearl S. Buck

POSITIVE ASPECTS OF AGING

Your attitude is important, so if you're going to live a long life you'll have to focus on the positive aspects of aging. Consider these advantages to living for a long time.

- You've had time to develop experience in all aspects of life. This should reduce the stress of daily living. You know what life is about and how to deal with it. Whatever happens, you've had some experience that you can relate to it.

- You continue to develop wisdom. If we look to the dictionary to define wisdom, we first must define wise. To be wise is to have the power of discerning and judging properly as to what is true or right. Wisdom is the quality or state of being wise. It takes a lifetime to truly develop wisdom; to have the experience to be able to discern what is true or right in life's complex challenges. It is the elders in a society that have sufficient life experience to bring to bear on a tricky situation to make a wise decision. This does not, however, happen automatically. Without conscious effort, the old may just become inflexible, narrow minded and opinionated.

- As you reach maturity, you care less about how others judge you. You are freer to be who you are. You become more authentic. You live your life by the principles you believe in and worry less about what others think. After all, you've had enough experience to decide for yourself.

- You have time to pursue special interests. When you were working and raising a family, you may not have had time to paint, or write, or learn to play the piano. Now, however, you have time to do the things you put off for later. Now, it's later. Go ahead and do it. You have the freedom to do the things you want to do.

- You have more time for friends. Now that you don't have to be so concerned about the job and the children, you have more time to visit with friends. You might even want to travel with them. Visiting a place of interest with friends can heighten the experience and the sense of connection to others.

- You have a better understanding of yourself. You've lived with yourself for several decades—long enough to understand who you are and how you want to live your life. You know what's important to you and you don't have to waste time with the unimportant or the trivial.

- Your intellect and curiosity may increase with age. You have time to investigate special interests and to increase your knowledge and intellect. As you learn more, you

Old age is not a matter for sorrow. It is a matter for thanks if we have left our work done behind us.
Thomas Carlyle

Some men are born old, and some men never seem so. If we keep well and cheerful, we are always young and at last die in youth even when in years would count as old.
Tryon Edwards

become more curious about the things you do not yet know or understand.

- Creativity is often heightened as you age. You aren't as concerned about the opinions of others and thus feel more free to express yourself in more diverse ways. So what if you look silly dancing. Who really cares? It doesn't matter if your painting doesn't really look like a tree, a flower or a person. Neither did Picasso's.

- You have time to devote to a cause. Volunteer to do something that you believe in—an environmental project, a political candidate, literacy, mentoring a child, or whatever is important to you. You have much to contribute to your community and to the world.

- You become more grateful for the little things in life—a smile, a flower, the sunset, a warm day, a child's playfulness, a friend's phone call, the absence of pain. The list is so long that you might want to start a gratitude journal to remind yourself of all the things you have to be grateful for.

- You can laugh at things that you formerly took too seriously. So what if a clerk was rude. It doesn't have to spoil your day. Just laugh because she looked so silly in her rudeness.

- Most people lose their fear of death after they pass middle age. You come to terms with the end of life. You deepen your spirituality and begin to view death as another step in the process of living and dying. This allows you to better appreciate each day remaining in your life.

- Your grandchildren come to visit. What greater delight can you have than to interact with children you love. Grandchildren allow you to enjoy the spirit of youth and when they begin to tire you out, they go home. You get the benefits without the responsibility. What could be better?

- Your ability to cope with distress increases and your stress level decreases. You've seen it all before and know that you can handle it.

- You have the freedom to do what you want. You don't have to set the alarm for 5:30 AM; you don't have to go to work; you don't have to cook and clean for the family. You have much more freedom to determine the course of your day and of your life.

To be happy, we must be true to nature, and carry our age along with us.
William Hazlitt

Old age equalizes—we are aware that what is happening to us has happened to untold numbers from the beginning of time. When we are young we act as if we were the first young people in the world.
Eric Hoffer

You have the choice to focus on the advantages of aging or the disadvantages. If you want to live long and happily, I'd recommend choosing to focus on what's good about living. Every phase of life has its own good points and those we'd rather skip, but happy living, at any time, requires that we place our attention on what makes us happy. The choice is yours.

The complete life, the perfect pattern, includes old age as well as youth and maturity. The beauty of the morning and the radiance of noon are good, but it would be a very silly person who drew the curtains and turned on the light in order to shut out the tranquility of the evening.
W. Somerset Maugham

ARE YOU OLD?

Age is pretty much a state of mind. Oh, I know that you can't change your chronological age, but you can choose to be old or to be young in thought. George Bush parachuted out of an airplane for the first time at 72. John Glenn took a trip into space at 78. You can probably think of examples of others who continued to think young regardless of their age.

Take for example, Bert who was 79 when he went to college. He'd always wanted to go to college, but had missed out when he was younger. Somehow the responsibilities of life always interfered. At 79, he decided that he was going to get older whether he went to college, or not. So he spent the last years of his life attending classes with students young enough to be his great grandchildren. He was an inspiration to them and an example of living your dream.

Your attitude is everything in aging. I hate to sound redundant, but this is perhaps the most important point in this book. Review these tips for maintaining a positive attitude.

- Be flexible—don't become rigid in your thinking.
- Undertake new challenges—learn something new.
- Respect your own opinion.
- Experience your pain and loss and then let go of the suffering.
- Take good care of yourself by eating nutritious food and exercising.
- Stay alert by exercising your brain.

- Take risks—do something new and different.
- Challenge society's myths about aging especially as they relate to you.
- Focus on the good things about getting older.
- Enjoy your grandchildren.
- Foster your spirituality, your relationship to your God and to the universe.
- Spend time with friends.
- Contribute to your community by volunteering to do something that you believe is important.
- Ignore your chronological age. Think young.
- Want to live a long life. Take adversity in stride. Sometimes people seem to die because they just get tired of living.
- Relax and enjoy life. Revel in the day-to-day experiences.
- Love yourself and others.
- Focus on success and the positive things in life. Focus on what you can do, rather than what you can't do.
- Foster your sense of humor. Laugh frequently.

Old age is ready to undertake tasks that youth shirked because they would take too long.
W. Somerset Maugham

AGING WELL

How committed are you to aging well? Are you committed enough to develop a plan and follow it? Knowing what to do is only the first step. If you've gotten this far in this book, you know what you need to do, but that won't help unless you actually apply what you've learned. You need to develop a plan. A form to help you is provided, beginning on page 106.

As you work on your plan, remember these points.

Don't just count your years, make your years count.
Ernest Meyers

- Physical exercise is among the most important things you can do to age well. Consider the three aspects of exercise—aerobics, weights, and flexibility. Walking is a wonderful way to start, if you are not accustomed to exercising.
- Plan to eat a nutritious diet, high in fiber and low in fat. Include lots of fish, vegetables, fruits, nuts, and whole grains. Reduce sugars and foods the body readily con-

verts to sugar. Stay informed about the newest findings since we're constantly learning new things about good nutrition.

- Maintain a healthy weight but, don't succumb to the latest fad diet. See the Body Mass Index in Chapter 2 to determine a good weight for you. When you reach your target weight, stay there. Continuous cycles of weight loss/gain are not good for your health.
- Don't expect pills to take care of all your problems.
- Don't smoke!! If you do smoke, find a way to quit.
- Develop and maintain a strong social support network. Include friends, family, and colleagues.
- Continuously learn new things. Challenge your brain; keep it active. You can and should learn throughout your life.
- Develop a sound financial plan. Know how much money you will need and take steps to assure that you will not run out.
- Drink in moderation or not at all. If you're going to drink, remember that red wine is filled with antioxidants.
- Meditate, pray, or spend quiet time in reflection. Growing spiritually is one of the benefits of aging.
- Continue to set and meet goals, both short term and long term. This is a way to add purpose and meaning to life.
- Do something for others. It's good for the heart and soul.
- Maintain a positive attitude. Stay flexible and adaptable. Remember that change is a part of living.

Live your life and forget your age.
Norman Vincent Peale

As for old age, embrace and love it. It abounds with pleasure if you know how to use it. The gradually declining years are among the sweetest in a man's life, and I maintain that, even when they have reached the extreme limit, they have their pleasure still.
Seneca

As you think about planning for the rest of your life, you might want to heed these words from an 82 year-old man who was dying, and accepting his impending death. This may be familiar to you, but it is worth a reminder.

If I Had My Life to Live Over

- I'd make more mistakes next time.
- I would relax, I would limber up.
- I would be crazier than I've been this trip.
- I know very few things I'd take seriously anymore.
- I would take more chances. I would take more trips.

- I would scale more mountains. I would swim more rivers.
- I would watch more sunsets.
- I would eat more ice cream and fewer beans.
- I would have more actual troubles and fewer imaginary ones.

It takes a long time to become young.
Pablo Picasso

You see . . . I was one of those people who lived pro-phylactically and sensibly, hour after hour and day after day. Oh, I've had my moments, and if I had to do it all over again, I'd have many more of them. In fact, I'd try not to have anything else, just moments, one after another. I've been one of those people who never went anywhere with-out a thermometer, a hot water bottle, a raincoat and a parachute. If I had it to do all over again, I'd travel lighter. I would start barefoot earlier in the spring, and stay that way later in the fall. And I would ride more merry-go-rounds, catch more gold rings, greet more people, pick more flowers, and dance more often . . . If I had it to do all over again, but you see, I don't.[73]

Remember this advice as you use the planning form on the following pages to develop your own personal plan for aging well.

Use these steps to complete your plan:

Old age though despised, is coveted by all.
Proverb

1. Think carefully about what your goal is in each area—physical, mental, social-emotional, spiritual, financial and humor. Write your goal in the space provided at the top of the page.

2. Review the tips in each chapter of this book and use them as a guide to help you select strategies that will help you reach your goals. These tips are summarized in this section to jog your memory. Write these, or other ideas, in the space for strategies. Write only those things that you will commit to actually doing. For example, don't say that you'll walk five miles per day, if exercising is new for you. You might want to start with one mile per day, three days per week. After you've done that successfully for several weeks, you might want to in-crease the distance and the number of days per week.

3. Decide when you will do each of the strategies that you've selected. For example, your walk might be be-

fore breakfast each day. Or it might be in the afternoon. It is probably best not to do strenuous exercise just before bedtime.

4. Where will you do it? On the treadmill or around the neighborhood? If your plan is to walk outside, what will you do if the weather is bad? Write it down.

5. What do you need to be successful? If you're going to use a treadmill for walking, then you'll need a treadmill. Or if you need a friend to walk with you, write it down and then make sure you get someone to walk with.

A graceful and honorable old age is the childhood of immortality.
Pindar
Greek Poet

Make a genuine commitment to yourself to follow your plan. Set your goals to stretch and challenge yourself, but they shouldn't be so difficult that you'll get discouraged. Improve your diet, get more serious about exercise, strengthen your social life. Engage in activities that challenge your brain, deepen your spirituality and put more laughter into your life.

Start by extending yourself a little. Achieve your goals and then stretch yourself a little more. Attaining your goals will motivate you to do more. Make a commitment to improving your life, for the rest of your life.

Use this planning process to help you create those life affirming habits—to help you develop life patterns that will help you age more successfully.

CONCLUSION

The person who has lived the most is not the one with the most years but the one with the richest experiences.
Jean Jacques Rousseau

I've given you what, I think, is the most important information that you will need to age with enthusiasm, grace and dignity. This information is worthless unless you make use of it. For example, most people know the basics of a good nutritious diet, but many don't apply that knowledge. Tips and suggestions are given throughout this book and planning forms are included in this chapter.

If you need additional assistance, Life Strategies, Inc. offers seminars, workbooks and personal coaching that will provide greater guidance.

Make use of whatever resources are available to you and take charge of your life. Don't just let life happen to you. Establish habits and patterns that will facilitate your aging with enthusiasm, grace and dignity. Use what you know to make your remaining years the best they can be. Good luck and good living.

Getting old is a fascination thing. The older you get, the older you want to get.
Keith Richards

Strategies to Maximize My Life
Planning Form

WHAT I AM COMMITTED TO DOING:	WHEN	WHERE	I NEED
Physical Goal:			
Physical Strategies:			
1.			
2.			
3.			
4.			
5.			

TIPS FOR STAYING PHYSICALLY HEALTHY

1. **Practice good nutrition**
    a. Eat nutritious foods that are low in fat and sugar.
    b. Take supplements to further enhance nutrition.
    c. Give yourself incentives for doing well.
2. **Exercise** and include the three crucial aspects
    a. Aerobic
    b. Weight training
    c. Flexibility
3. **If you smoke, quit!** Smoking is more hazardous to your health than almost anything else you can do.
4. **Associate with others who practice the healthy habits** that you're working toward.
5. **Visualize** yourself the way you want to be.
6. **Use alcohol in moderation** and know the benefits of red wine.
7. **Keep stress to a minimum.** Practice stress reduction techniques, including:
    a. Meditation
    b. Yoga
    c. Self hypnosis
    d. Tai Chi
8. **Maintain a healthy weight.** Obesity causes a multitude of health problems.
9. **Maintain a sense of humor.** Laugh loudly and often.
10. **Maintain a positive attitude.** You create the quality of your life in your mind, so see the world in a positive way.
11. **Stay active!** View activity as a good thing and keep moving.

WHAT I AM COMMITTED TO DOING:	WHEN	WHERE	I NEED
Mental Goal:			
Mental Strategies:			
1.			
2.			
3.			
4.			
5.			

WAYS TO MAINTAIN MENTAL ACUMEN

1. **Maintain a positive attitude.** Don't let a negative attitude become a self-fulfilling prophecy.

2. **Take a class** that is challenging and interesting to you. Learn a new skill or more about something that you want to know.

3. **Play games.** Games like bridge, chess, or Scrabble are particularly good for mental stimulation, but lots of other games are also good for keeping you mentally engaged and interacting with others.

4. **Do puzzles** of all kinds. Crossword puzzles, jigsaw puzzles, logic puzzles, and visual-spatial puzzles, as well as others, will stimulate your brain cells.

5. **Nurture social relationships.** They keep you engaged with others and give you opportunities to use mental skills.

6. **Volunteer your time.** Get involved with a cause that you believe is important.

7. **Seek variety and challenge** in your life. Don't become too comfortable.

8. **Turn off the TV.** Watching television is relaxing and easy, and that's the problem; it's too easy.

9. **Read.** Reading is a wonderful alternative to watching television. It's entertaining and informative. It is a great way to challenge your ideas and make you think.

10. **Join or start a book club.** Discussions with others about a book that you all read is a stimulating and challenging way to read and learn from others.

11. **Write something.** Writing is an outstanding way to force yourself to clarify your thinking. Write letters to friends and family. You might even write your autobiography. Consider writing poetry, short stories, or even a novel.

12. **Continue to learn** throughout your life. Your can learn new things by reading, searching the web, taking a class, or talking to others knowledgeable about a topic.

13. **Remain physically active.** Get lots of exercise. Walk, ride a bike, play with your grandchildren, take an exercise class, work in the garden, lift weights. Do something, anything, that keeps you up and moving!

14. **Avoid head injuries.** Drive a car with airbags. Buckle your seat belt. Wear a helmet when you ride your bike or engage in other activities in which you might fall on your head.

15. **Keep working at a job.** This doesn't have to be a full time job—you can do something part time. Work at something that will keep you challenged and mentally engaged.

16. **Meditate** or practice other stress reduction techniques. Chronic stress alters brain structure and impairs cognitive function.

17. **Seek help for depression** or other emotional disorders.

18. **Effectively control high blood pressure, diabetes, high cholesterol, and other medical ailments.** Poor physical health can have a detrimental effect on the brain.

19. **Learn something entirely new** like playing a musical instrument, ballroom dancing, painting, knitting, or how to use a computer or the internet.

20. **Go to the library.** Investigate new areas. Browse in an area of the library that you might not have thought about before.

WHAT I AM COMMITTED TO DOING:	WHEN	WHERE	I NEED
Social-Emotional Goal:			
Social-Emotional Strategies:			
1.			
2.			
3.			
4.			
5.			

TIPS FOR INCREASING SOCIAL CONTACT

1. **Maintain and enhance a positive attitude.** This will go a long way in increasing social contact. It's more pleasant to be around someone who is positive and cheerful.

2. **Maintain and enhance your sense of humor.** Laughing is good for you and stimulates good relationships.

3. **Invite someone to lunch**—either in your home or in a restaurant.

4. **Call your sister**/brother/a friend just to say hello.

5. **Join community organizations.** This will get you involved with a group of people on a regular basis.

6. **Join a religious group.** These provide a multitude of opportunities to interact with others in a variety of ways.

7. **Go on a trip** with your spouse, a friend, or a group.

8. **Take a class** in something that interests you. You can do this at the local community college, the local school district community education program, or other places in your community. Check the local newspaper, the yellow pages, ask a neighbor or look in the mail for community education flyers.

9. **Get a part-time job.** Earn some money for using your skills and talents and meet some new people in the process. You can do something on a part time basis that interests you, but you couldn't do when you were younger because it wouldn't support you and your family.

10. **Volunteer your time** doing something that is of particular interest to you. Volunteerism is an outstanding way to meet new people and to gain a sense of making a contribution.

11. **Start a neighborhood bridge** (or some other card game) **group.** Or this could be walking, or crafts, or anything that interests you and others in your neighborhood. It could be gourmet cooking, monthly dinner gatherings in a local restaurant—the possibilities are endless.

12. **Spend more time with your grandchildren.** Take them on a trip. Invite them to spend the weekend with you. Grandchildren will lift your spirits better than anyone else can. This is good for your grandchildren, as well as for you. It will give them enduring lifetime memories of grandma or grandpa.

13. **Do something silly.** It's good to be able to laugh at yourself. We tend to take ourselves too seriously. Life should be fun.

14. **Do errands for a sick friend.** It will be good for you as well as your friend.

15. Make a special effort to **keep in contact with young people.** It will expand your thinking and help you see the world through the eyes of others who are younger.

16. **Build up your tolerance for being alone.** As you get older, it is likely that you will spend more time alone. Being alone gives you time for reading, reflection, writing, hobbies, or whatever you enjoy that doesn't require interaction with someone else.

17. **Get a pet,** especially if you live alone. Pets provide many of the same benefits as human relationships.

18. **Work in the garden.** Interaction with living things of any kind provides benefits.

WHAT I AM COMMITTED TO DOING:	WHEN	WHERE	I NEED
Spiritual Goal:			
Spiritual Strategies:			
1.			
2.			
3.			
4.			
5.			

WAYS TO GROW SPIRITUALLY

1. **Join a prayer group** that may, or may not, be associated with a religious organization.

2. **Meditate** regularly for at least twenty minutes and work up to longer periods.

3. **Write your autobiography.** What was important about your life? What were the important events that helped shape who you are? Use this task to help you reflect on your life and its meaning.

4. **Seek ways to give back** to your community. What kind of volunteer work is needed where you live? What would you feel good about contributing?

5. **Put together a photograph album that depicts your life.** You might use this in conjunction with your autobiography.

6. **Compile the family genealogy or write a family history.** Emphasize the strengths, courage and contributions of your family.

7. **Tape your memoirs**—either audio or video.

8. **Use an art medium to express yourself.** You might choose sculpture, oil painting, drawing, music or whatever you prefer.

9. **Live in the present moment.** The present is the only time that you have. The past is over and the future hasn't yet arrived.

10. **Understand and accept who you are.** Everyone has both strengths and weaknesses. Accept them. No one is perfect.

11. **Love.** Increase the love in your life. Pay attention to those you love and expand that love to more people. Make peace with anyone in your life with whom you are not at peace. Practice unconditional love—love that doesn't require anything in return.

WHAT I AM COMMITTED TO DOING:	WHEN	WHERE	I NEED
Financial Goal:			
Financial Strategies:			
1.			
2.			
3.			
4.			
5.			

DEVELOPING A FINANCIAL PLAN

Whether you work with a financial planner or do it on your own, you'll need answers to the questions below. If you can't answer them, consider putting the process of answering them into your plan.

1. What are your goals? Long term and short term?
2. At what age do you expect to retire?
3. What do you anticipate your annual income will need to be when you retire? Will you have a pension?
4. What assets do you have? List all your assets -savings, investments, house, car, possessions.
5. What liabilities do you have? What bills do you owe—house, car, credit cards, other?
6. How many dependents do you have? Do any of your dependents have conditions that might require extra financial expenditures?
7. Do you anticipate any large expenses in the future?
8. How involved do you want to be in making investment decisions? Be *very* careful about giving your advisor too much control over your money.
9. How great is your tolerance for risk? Do you want your money to be invested very conservatively or do you have a higher tolerance for risk?

After you've answered these questions, your financial plan will incorporate the strategies you're going to follow to acquire the funds you'll need. If you're going to work with a financial planner, you should develop a plan for securing one who is reputable and with whom you can work comfortably.

WHAT I AM COMMITTED TO DOING:	WHEN	WHERE	I NEED
Humor Goal:			
Humor Strategies:			
1.			
2.			
3.			
4.			
5.			

WAYS TO PUT MORE LAUGHTER INTO YOUR LIFE

1. Read the comics and cartoons in the newspaper.
2. Watch funny programs on television.
3. Get joke books from the library and read them.
4. Browse through the humor section at a bookstore.
5. Collect jokes from your friends.
6. Tell jokes, even if you don't do it well. You'll get better with practice. If you can laugh at yourself, it might even be funnier to tell it badly.
7. Explore humor sites on the web.
8. Post your favorite cartoons on the refrigerator.
9. Go to humorous movies.
10. Act silly. Do something that you don't usually do, just for fun.
11. Tell jokes with your grandchildren.
12. Laugh when other people tell jokes. Sometimes even laugh at how bad they are.
13. Listen to audio tapes of comedians when you're in the car.
14. Play and laugh with your grandchildren.
15. Laugh at yourself. Take life more lightly.
16. Laugh at your mistakes. The vast majority of the mistakes we make are not in the important things of life and probably should be laughed at.
17. Practice looking at the funny side of stressful events. It's easier to laugh about the soup boiling over than to stress out about it.
18. Laugh at aging. If you can exaggerate and laugh about the changes that you're experiencing as you get older, it doesn't seem so bad.

RESOURCES

1. AARP
    601 E Street
    Washington, DC 20049
    Toll Free: (800)424-3410
    Phone: (202)434-2277
    Website: www.aarp.org
2. Administration on Aging (AoA)
    330 Independence Avenue, SW
    Washington, DC 20201
    Phone: (202)619-7501
    Email: AoAInfo@aoa.gov
    Website: www.aoa.gov
3. Alzheimer's Association
    919 North Michigan Ave.
    Suite 1100
    Chicago, IL 60611-1676
    Toll Free: (800)272-3900
    Phone: (312)335-8700
    Fax: (312)335-1110
    Email: info@alz.org
    Website: www.alz.org
4. Alzheimer's Disease Education and Referral (ADEAR) Center
    PO Box 8250
    Silver Spring, MD 20907-8250
    Toll Free: (800)438-4380
    Email: adear@alzheimers.org
    Website: http://www.alzheimers.org
5. American Association for Geriatric Psychiatry
    7910 Woodmont Avenue, Suite 1050
    Bethesda, Maryland 20814
    (301)654-7850

Fax: (301)654-4137
Email: main@aagpgpa.org
Website: www.aagpgpa.org

6. American Society on Aging (ASoA)
   833 Market Street
   Suite 511
   San Francisco, CA 94103-1824
   Phone: (415)974-9600
   Email: info@asaging.org
   Website: www.asaging.org

7. Center for Disease Control (CDC)
   1600 Clifton Road
   Atlanta, GA 30333
   (404)639-3311
   Public Inquires: (800)311-3435 or (404)639-3534
   Website: www.cdc.gov

8. American Federation for Aging Research (AFAR)
   70 West 40th Street
   11th Floor
   New York, NY 10018
   Phone: (212)703-9977
   Fax: (212)997-0330
   Email: amfedaging@aol.com
   Website: www.afar.org

9. Continuing Medical Education, Inc. (CME, Inc.)
   2801 McGaw Avenue
   Irvine, CA 92614-5835
   Toll Free: (800)933-2632
   Phone: (949)250-1008
   Website: www.cmeinc.com

10. National Institute on Aging (NIA)
    Building 31, Room 5C27
    31 Center Drive, MSC2292
    Bethesda, MS 20892
    Phone: (301)496-1752
    Website: www.nia.nih.gov

11. Spiritual Eldering Institute
    970 Aurora Avenue
    Boulder, CO 80302
    Phone: (303)449-7243
    Fax: (303)938-1277
    Email: info@spiritualeldering.org
    Website: www.spiritualeldering.org

RESOURCES—FINANCIAL PLANNERS:

To find a financial planner in your area, contact one of these organizations:
(These are professional associations for financial planners. I offer them as a resource, but do not guarantee the results you will obtain through the use of any of these organizations.)

1. American Institute of Certified Public Accountants-Personal Financial Planning Division
    Harborside Financial Center
    201 Plaza 3
    Jersey City, NJ 07311-3881
    Toll Free: (800)862-4272, (888)777-7077
    www.aicpa.org
2. Certified Financial Planner Board of Standards
    1700 Broadway, Suite 2100
    Denver, CO 80290-2101
    Toll Free: (888)-CFP-MARK
    Website: www.cfp-board.org
3. Financial Planning Association
    Atlanta Office: 5775 Glenridge Drive, NE
                       Suite B-300
                       Atlanta, GA 30328
    Denver Office: 3801 E. Florida Avenue
                       Suite 708
                       Denver, CO 80210
    Washington, DC Office   1615 L Street, NW
                       Suite 650
                       Washington, DC 20036
    Toll Free: (800)945-4237, (800)322-4237
    Website: www.fpanet.org
4. National Association of Personal Financial Advisors
    355 W. Dundee Road, Suite 200
    Buffalo Grove, IL 60089
    Toll Free: (888)FEE-ONLY
    www.napfa.org
5. Society of Financial Service Professionals
    270 South Bryn Mawr Avenue
    Bryn Mawr, PA 19010-2195
    Phone: (610)526-2500
    Website: www.financialpro.org

BIBLIOGRAPHY

1. "Aging of the Brain," http://hme.mira.net.
2. "Aging, Exercise, and Depression: Separating Myths From Reality," The Medical Reporter, http://medicalreporter.health.org.
3. "Aging Well," Administration on Aging, www.aoa.dhhs.gov.
4. Agronin, Marc E., M.D.; "Addressing Sexuality and Sexual Dysfunction", Geriatric Times, January/February 2001, Vol. II, Issue 1, www.medinfosource.com
5. Alexander, Dr. Taylor and Dr. Neena L. Chappell; "Volunteering and Healthy Aging: A Great Combination for Seniors," www.stridemagazine.com/2001
6. "Alzheimer's Disease: Am I at Risk?," Novartis. www.alzheimersdisease.com.
7. "Alzheimer's Disease and Apolipoprotein E," Texas Department of Health, www.tdh.state.tx.us, 2001.
8. Amerman, Don; "Sex and Aging: Easing Time's Impact on Performance and Enjoyment", Rockhill Communications, http://yourhealth.queens.org
9. "Anatomy of the Brain," American Health Assistance Foundation, www.ahaf.org.
10. "Antioxidants and Free Radicals," www.rice.edu
11. "Antioxidants + Exercise = Slow Aging", Source: HealthScout, 3/29/99, http://wealthforfreedom.com.
12. "Assessing Your Risk for Alzheimer's Disease (from the Mayo Clinic)" DetroitNow Healthy Living, WXYZ-TV Scripps Howard Broadcasting, Healthy Living Resources. www.detnow.com, 2000.
13. Associated Press. "Study Rates Estrogen Alternative." Health News, InteliHealth, Inc., April 19, 2001.
14. "The Benefits of Vitamin C," http://allergies.about.com.
15. Bennett, Michael L., Pharm.D., "Vanity Medicine," New Hope.com, Nutrition Science News, www.naturalinvestor.com.
16. Benson, Herbert, M.D.; "Examining the Faith Factor", www.vhl.org.
17. Berman, Jennifer, M.D. and Laura Berman; "FAQs on Female Sexual Dysfunction", University of California at Los Angeles, www.msnbc.com.
18. "Beta Carotene," Go Ask Alice, Columbia University's Health Question & Answer Internet Service, www.goaskalice.columbia.edu.
19. "Beta Carotene," Wellness Guide to Dietary Supplements," UC Berkeley Wellness, www.berkeleywellness.com.
20. Body Trends Health and Fitness, www.bodytrends.com.

21. Boeree, Dr. C. George; "Erik Erikson 1902–1994", 1997. www.ship.edu.

22. "Botox Injections," www.cosmeticsurgeryfyi.com.

23. "Calcium Benefits," University of Texas Southwestern Medical Center, www3.utsouthwestern.edu.

24. "Can I Live to Be 125?", Visions of the 21st Century, Time Media Kit, www.time.com.

25. "Can Walking and Socializing Protect Against Dementia?", Neurology Reviews.Com; www.neurologyreviews.com

26. "Canada's Aging Specialist Says Volunteering is a Secret Ingredient for Healthy Aging," October 28, 1999, www.volunteer.ca/volunteer/news

27. Carper, Jean; "Mixed Up About Nutrition?", USA Weekend, July 27–29, 2001.

28. Carter, Rosalynn with Susan K. Golant, *Helping Someone with Mental Illness*, Times Books Random House, 1998.

29. Carton, Emily, MA LISW, "Depression and Older Adults," Selfhelp Magazine, www.shpm.com.

30. Center for Disease Control, www.cdc.gov.

31. Challem, Jack, "Coenzyme Q10: It May Just Be the Miracle Vitamin of the 1990's," The Nutrition Reporter, www.thenutritionreporter.com.

32. Chippendale, Lisa; "Spirituality, Religion and Healthy Aging", www.infoaging.org.

33. "Choosing a Financial Advisor," New England Financial, www.nefn.com

34. "Chromium Picolinate," UC Berkeley Wellness, Wellness Guide to Dietary Supplements, www.berkeleywellness.com.

35. "Coenzyme Q10," Smart Nutrition, www.smart-drugs.com.

36. "Cognition, Aging and Nutrient Protocols," Health Science Research Institute, www.healthscience.com, 2001.

37. Cohn, Rabbi Edward Paul, "The Privilege of Aging," www.templesinaino.org/aging.

38. Cohen, Gene D. "Chapter 32: Aging and Mental Health" The Merck Manual of Geriatrics, www.merck.com, 2001.

39. Cohen, Gene D.; *The Creative Age*, Quill an Imprint of Harper Collins Publishers, New York, 2000.

40. Cooper, Desiree. "Fear Grows With Every Memory Lapse." Detroit Free Press. January, 2002.

41. "Coping with Depression and the Holidays," American Association for Geriatric Psychiatry.

42. Cutter, John A., "Spirituality may help people live longer," November 17, 1999. www.cnn.com.

43. Demeter, Deborah; "Sex and the Elderly", The Human Sexuality Web, www.umkc.edu.

44. Demko, David J. Ph.D., "Positive Lives Are Positively Longer", Age Venture News Service, www.demko.com.

45. Dersch, Charette A., Steven M. Harris, Thomas Kimball, James P. Marshall, Michael A. Negretti; "Sexual Issues for Aging Adults", Texas Tech University, www.hs.ttu.edu.

46. Dreyfuss, Ira. "Exercise May Help to Fight Mental Decline in Aging," C-Health, www.canoe.ca/Health0108.

47. Driskell, Judy A. Ph.D., R.D.; "Vitamin-Mineral Supplements and Their Usage by Adults", www.ianr.unl.edu.

48. Duyff, Roberta Larson, M.S., R.D., D.F.C.S., "Dietary Supplements—Some to Take, Some to Dump," National Health & Wellness Club, http://visitors.healthandwellnessclub.com.

49. Dychtwald, Ken and Joe Flower; *Age Wave*, Bantam Books, New York, 1990.

50. Dychtwald, Ken, "Aging in the 21st Century: Gerassic Park or Shangri-La?", Age Wave, LLC, www.asaging.org.

51. Engleman, Marge; *Aerobics of the Mind: Keeping the Mind Active in Aging*, Venture Publishing, Inc.; State College, Pennsylvania; 1996.

52. English, Jim and Dean Ward, M.D., "Viagra: Performance, Side Effects and Safe Alternatives," www.doctorg.com.

53. "Erikson's Development Stages", www.hcc.hawaii.edu,

54. "Fall Community Meeting 2000, Successful Aging: Fact or Fiction?", UCLA Center on Aging, www.aging.ucla.edu.

55. "Fat and Cholesterol in the Diet," http://jhhs.client.web-health.com.

56. "Fats, Blood Cholesterol, LDL, HDL: Know the Enemy," www.fatfreekitchen.com.

57. Fears, Carla, "When Depression Accompanies Aging," Meriter Senior Adult Services, www.meriter.com.

58. Financial Planner Interview Form, National Association of Personal Financial Advisors, www.planretire.com.

59. "Finding and Selecting a Financial Advisor," Forum for Investor Advice, www.investoradvice.org.

60. Fogler, Janet, and Lynn Stern; *Improving Your Memory: How to Remember What You're Starting to Forget*, The Johns Hopkins University Press, Baltimore and London, 1994.

61. "Forgetfulness: It's Not Always What You Think," New York State Office for the Aging, 2001. http://agingwell.state.ny.us.

62. Gascon, Dan; Humor for Your Health, www.humorforyourhealth.com.

63. "General Financial Skills Every Resident Needs," Association of American Medical Colleges, www.aamc.org.

64. Goldman, Robert, M.D., D.O., Ph.D., with Ronald Klatz, M.D., D.O., and Lisa Berger; Brain Fitness: *Anti-Aging Strategies for Achieving Super Mind Power*, Doubleday, New York, 1999.

65. "Hair Transplantation," www.cosmeticsurgeryfyi.com.

66. "Health Benefits of Selenium," SeleniumSelect, www.seleniumselect.com.

67. Hinder, Stan; How to Retire Happy, McGraw Hill, New York, 2001.

68. "How to Know You're Getting Older," www.seniors-site.com.

69. "How to Recognize Depression, Get Help, and Be Well Again," The National Council on the Aging and American Association or Geriatric Psychiatry.

70. "How to Talk to Your Doctor About Depression . . . and Be Well Again," The National Council on Aging and the American Association for Geriatric Psychiatry.

71. "Humor: How Does It Work?", Holistic-online.com, www.holistic-online.com.

72. "Identifying and Coping with Depression," Women & Aging Letter, www.aoa.gov.

73. "If I Had My Life To Live Over," Seniors-Site, www.seniors-site.com.

74. Jaret, Peter, "Life of the Party," WebMD Health, http://my.webmd.com.

75. Jennings, Peter, "21st Century Lives: James Hillman," ABC News Shows, http://abcnews.go.com.

76. Jones, Daniel P. and Leslie Barnes Fluharty, Ph. D.; "Information on Sexuality and Aging", The College of Wooster, www.wooster.edu.

77. Kaspari, Linda, "The Benefits of a B-Complex," www.focusnewsletter.org.

78. Kelder, Peter; *Ancient Secret of the Fountain of Youth*, Doubleday, New York, 1985.

79. Kendall, Ph.D., R.D., Pat. "Ginkgo Biloba: Wonder Herb for an Aging Brain?" The Diet Channel, www.thedietchannel.com, 1999.

80. Lemonick, Michael D. and Alice Park. "The Nun Study." *Time Magazine*, May 14, 2001, pp. 54–64.

81. Life Extension Foundation, www.lef.org.

82. "Life Extension Lifestyle," www.seniors-site.com.

83. "Looking Out for Depression," Elder Action: Action Ideas for Older Persons and Their Families, Administration on Aging, www.aoa.gov.

84. Lynn, Dorree, Ph.D., "Psychotherapy, Spirituality, and Aging", www.pariswoman.com.

85. Mahoney, David and Richard Restak, M.D., *The Longevity Strategy: How to Live to 100 Using the Brain-Body Connection*, John Wiley & Sons, Inc.,1998.

86. "Maintaining and Enhancing Cognitive Function in Later Life," *MindAlert*, A newsletter of the research project sponsored by MetLife Foundation and Archstone Foundation. www.asaging.org.

87. Maragopoulos, D., "Nutrition and Your Diet," FCFH Newsletter, Full Circle Family Health, Dec/Jan Newsletter, 1998. www.debfnp.com.

88. Mathieu, André, C.P., "Toward a Spirituality of Aging", www.cptryon.org.

89. McFarlane, Brent, "Cutting Edge Nutrition—Eating Your Way to Success," December 8, 1999; www.canthrow.com.

90. McGhee, Paul E., Ph.D.; "Humor and Health," Holistic-online.com, www.holistic-online.com.

91. Medical College of Georgia (MCG) Health System, www.mcghealthcare.org.

92. "Mental Health and Aging: Addressing the Unmet Needs of America's Elderly," First Gov for Seniors. www.seniors.gov/articles.

93. "Mental Wellness Tips." The Healthy Aging Campaign. Educational Television Network, Inc., 2001. www.healthyaging.net.

94. Mirkin, Gabe, M.D., "Alzheimer's Disease," www.drmirkin.com, 3/19/99.

95. Moorhead, Mary; "Successful Aging in the 21st Century", www.fina-a-therapist.com/articles.

96. Moran, MPH, Mark. "Older Adults Who Stay Social Have More Brain Power," WebMDHealth, http://my.webmd.com.

97. National Agriculture Library, www.nal.usda.gov.

98. National Heart, Lungs, Blood Institute, www.nhlbi.nih.gov.

99. National Institute for Mental Health, www.nimh.nih.gov.

100. Newberg, Andrew, M.D. and Eugene D'Aquili, M.D., Ph.D, and Vince Rause; *Why God Won't Go Away: Brain Science and the Biology of Belief*, Ballantine Books, New York, 2001.

101. "Nutrition, Health, and Disease", www.aoa.gov.

102. "Older Population by Age: 1900–2050—Percent 65+ and 85+," Administration on Aging, www.aoa.dhhs.gov/aoa/stats.

103. Oregon State University, www.orst.edu.

104. Pararas-Carayannis, Ph.D., George. "Memory/Cognitive Function Loss" December, 2000. www.geocities.com.

105. "Physical Activity and Good Nutrition: Essential Elements to Prevent Chronic Diseases and Obesity", www.cdc.gov.

106. "A Primer on Fats and Oils," www.eatright.org.

107. "Protect Your Money: Check Out Brokers and Advisors," U.S. Securities and Exchange Commission, www.sec.gov.

108. Raloff, J., "Boning up on calcium shouldn't be sporadic," Science News Online, www.sciencenews.org.

109. Redd, Darlyne; "Matters of the Heart and Mind: African American Elders and Grief", Summer 2001, www.asaging.org.

110. "Refine, Reshape, Restore: Cosmetic Surgery," Straith Clinic, Bingham Farms, Michigan.

111. "Remaining active, productive the key to successful aging", Baycrest Report on Healthy Aging, Baycrest Centre for Geriatric Care.

112. "Retirement Planning and Volunteerism," Helpguide.org: Where to Turn for Help," www.helpguide.org.

113. Rowe, John W. M.D. and Robert L. Kahn, Ph.D. *Successful Aging*, Dell Publishing, New York, New York, 1998.

114. Rubin, Rita. "Estrogen Alternative Doesn't Protect Mental Function." www.usatoday.com, USA Today, 2001.

115. Scemons, Donna, RN, MSN, MA, CETN,CNS; "Death and Humor", Nursing Home Medicine, www.mmhc.com.

116. "Scientists Provide Strategies for Maintaining Cognitive Vitality in Old Age" News Release of Institute for the Study of Aging. www.aging-institute.org, March 15, 2001.

117. Sehl, Mark, M.D., "Aging Can Be a Positive Experience," www.marksehl.com.

118. Seniors' Health, "Expert Commentary: Sexuality and Aging", February 15, 1999, www.intelihealth.com.

119. "Seniors Volunteer for Longer Life," www.demdo.com.

120. Severson, Lucky. "Alzheimer's Disease—Mental Stimulation Delays Onset" http://pspinformation.com, 1999–2000.

121. "Sexual Response and Aging", Engender Health, www.engenderhealth.org.

122. "Sexuality in Later Life", www.wellnessweb.com , www.agepage.com.

123. Sheehy, Gail; New Passages, Balentine Books, New York, 1995.

124. Sherret, P.J., "DHEA: Ignore the Hype," Quack Watch, www.quackwatch.com.

125. Sinnamon, The Rev. Ms. Sue E., "Spirituality and Aging", March 25, 2001, http://ucevanston.org.

126. Smith, Mary Helen and Shuford; *The Retirement Sourcebook*, Roxbury Park Lowell House, Los Angeles, 1999.

127. Smith, Mary Helen and Shuford; *101 Secrets for a Great Retirement*, Roxbury Park Lowell House, Los Angeles, 2000.

128. Sobel, David S. M.DS., MPH and Robert Ornstein, Ph.D.; "Good Humor, Good Health," Kaiser Permanente, www.kaiserpermanente.org.

129. "Social Wellness Tips: Secrets for Healthy Aging", The Healthy Aging Campaign, www.healthyaging.net.

130. "Spirituality and Aging," www.emanu-el.org.

131. "Spirituality and Aging", http://iml.umkc.edu.

132. "Symptoms," Alzheimer's Association. www.alz.org, 2001.

133. Taylor, Nigel Brian, CFP; "Checking up on Your Financial Planner," Nigel B. Taylor & Associates, www.protectassets.com.

134. "10 Questions to Ask When Choosing a Financial Planner," Certified Financial Planner Board of Standards, www.cfp-board.org.

135. "Therapeutic Benefits of Laughter," Holistic-online.com, www.holistic-online.com.

136. Thompson, April. "Inside the Brain: New Research Prescribes Mental Exercise." American Society on Aging, www.asaging.org.

137. "The Truth About Sex and Aging", March 1998, www.healthcare.ucla.edu.

138. Transcendental Meditation Program, www.tm.org.

139. "Understanding Free Radicals and Antioxidants," HealthCheck Systems, www.healthchecksystems.com.

140. University of Buffalo, www.buffalo.edu.

141. University of Nebraska at Lincoln, www.ianr.unl.edu.

142. VanTine, Julia, Bridget Doherty, and the Editors of Prevention Health Books for Women; *Growing Younger: Breakthrough Age-Defying Secrets*, Rodale, 1999.

143. "Viagra Information," www.all-viagra.com.

144. "Viagra Research (clinical trials)," www.impotence-causes-treatment-male-sexual-dysfunction.com.

145. "Viagra Side Effects: Not Just a Medical Problem," ABC News, http://abcnews.go.com.

146. "Vitamin B Complex," Whole Health Discount Center, www.health-pages.com.

147. "Vitamins C and E: Protection Against Mental Decline," MCW Health Link, http://healthlink.mcw.edu, Medical College of Wisconsin, 2001.

148. "The Vitamin C Controversy," Life Extension Foundation, www.lef.org.

149. "Vit C Supplementation," www.acu-cell.com.

150. "The Vitamin E Factor," vitamine-factor.com.

151. "Vitamin E," Wellness Guide to Dietary Supplements, UC Berkeley Wellness, www.berkleywellness.com.

152. "Volunteer Opportunities," New York State Office for the Aging, http://agingwell.state.ny.us/center/volunteer/index.htm.

153. "What Are the Benefits of Vitamins and Phytochemicals?," WebMD Health, http://my.webmd.com.

154. "What Are the Viagra Side Effects," www.drug-side-effects.org.

155. "What You Should Know About Financial Planning," Certified Financial Planner Board of Standards, www.cfp-board.org.

156. Wooten, Patty; "Humor: an Antidote for Stress," Jest for the Health of It, Articles About Therapeutic Humor, www.jesthealth.com.

INDEX